A GUIDE TO THE INDU
OF NORTHAM
2nd Ed

C000149458

Compiled on behalf of Northamptonshire Industria
    Peter Perkins
    Geoffrey Starmer
    Barry Taylor

The Compilers of the 1st Edition were Peter Perkins, Roy Sheffield and Geoffrey Starmer.

CONTENTS

Published by John Stanley Publishers on behalf of Northamptonshire Industrial Archaeology Group.
ISBN No: 978 1 905781 00 3

Cover photos:
Front upper Left: *Tram shelter, Northampton* (Site 259);   Right: *Canal bridge, Cosgrove* (Site 74)
Front lower Left: *Newman's shoe factory, Kettering* (Site 205);   Right: *Wellingborough station* (Site 427)
Back   Left: *National Lift Tower, Northampton* (Site 312);   Right: *Water tower, Finedon* (Site 125)

PREFACE

The physical evidence of Northamptonshire's industrial past is fast disappearing. This Guide has been produced by NIAG to increase awareness of what remains. It aims to be of interest to both general readers and industrial archaeologists. The Guide is not an exhaustive list of all industrial sites in the county. In certain categories the Compilers have necessarily chosen a representative sample and in many respects it has been a personal choice. This is particularly true in industries such as boot & shoe for which the county is justly famous. Despite the rapid decline of the industry over the past 50 years, there remain a large number of buildings relating to the industry. Our selection has been made largely on the basis of historical significance and architectural interest.

The main criteria for inclusion of a site in the Guide is that some physical evidence of the site remains, either through structure or earthwork. While the majority of sites pertain to the industrial period since 1750, earlier sites are included where relevant, for example medieval road bridges. Although we have excluded most sites post-1945, there is one notable exception - the former Express Lift Tower (now called the National Lift Tower) in Northampton. We have chosen to cover industrial heritage in its widest sense. The more obvious forms include features associated with transport, manufacturing and quarrying. Perhaps less obvious are some of the service industries and the different forms of entertainment such as cinemas and theatres. We have excluded agricultural sites where there is no specific industrial connection.

INDUSTRIAL DEVELOPMENT IN NORTHAMPTONSHIRE

Compared with its northern neighbours, Northamptonshire's lack of coal retarded its large-scale industrial development. Despite this, from early times there have been a variety of industrial developments in the county.

Extractive industries
The natural resources of Northamptonshire are stone, clay and iron ore. Quarrying of stone for building has been carried out at a number of places, and was recorded at Weldon as early as the

Tramways at Loddington ironstone quarries in 1958

13th century (13thC). Later, the stone here was worked underground as was stone for slates at Collyweston. The once famous quarries at Helmdon are remembered in a 14thC stained glass window showing a stone mason. As well as stone for building, limestone was quarried for burning in kilns for agricultural as well as building purposes. Over 30 kilns were at work in the county in the 1920s. There was only one cement works in the county, which traded as the Premier Portland Cement Co. Ltd. at Irthlingborough. There are records of over 200 brickyards although most were quite small. The yards were usually in open country near the larger towns but their sites have been obliterated by urban development. Ruined kilns can still be found at some of the smaller rural yards.

2

Despite the smelting of Northamptonshire iron ore in pre-Roman times, its existence was later forgotten until it aroused interest at the Great Exhibition of 1851. Following demonstrations that the ore could be smelted satisfactorily, the iron ore industry developed in the county and continued until the 1960s when most of the remaining quarries closed, leaving those serving Corby ironworks to survive until 1980. Although the majority of iron ore extraction was open-cast, there were some underground workings and some survive although they are inaccessible. Most of the open-cast workings have been restored or used for landfill, except for a few instances, such as in the country parks at Irchester, Hunsbury Hill and Twywell.

Some of the ore extracted went out-of-county for smelting; however, from the mid-19thC there were blast furnaces at 12 sites in the county, although not all were operating at the same time. In the 1930s Stewarts & Lloyds Ltd. created an integrated iron, steel and tube works at Corby with a new township of some 2200 houses. Iron and steel production at Corby ended in 1980 although the tube works remains in operation.

Processing the products of the land

Farming and forestry were practised extensively in the county. The subsequent processing of the products of these led to significant structures such as flour mills, maltings, tanneries and saw-mills. The river systems of Northamptonshire provided power at over 170 sites. None are now at work and many have been demolished. Although a few have machinery inside, most of the survivors have been converted to dwellings.

Watermill at Thrapston in early 20thC

Windmills were introduced in the 12thC. Nearly 200 windmill sites have been identified in Northamptonshire although not all would have had a windmill at any given time. There are no remains of post mills and of the 12 upstanding remains of tower mills, some have been so altered by additions for house conversion that they are hardly recognisable. In 1788 a Boulton & Watt steam engine was installed in the watermill at Sulgrave. This was the first steam engine in the county (the second, another Boulton & Watt engine, was not erected until 1797 at the Cotton Mill, Northampton). During the 19thC, other mills began to use steam engines as supplementary power and by 1886 eight mills were entirely dependent on steam.

Barley was milled for animal food but it was also converted to malt for brewing. The increase in size of the common brewers in towns led to the construction of large maltings nearby, resulting in the closure of the small rural maltings, which were soon adapted for other purposes and lost their distinctive conical or pyramidal roofs. Some of the larger town maltings survive and despite adaptation for other use, still retain characteristic features as can be seen at Kettering and Oundle.

Leather is produced from the skins and hides of animals. Early tanning methods took a long time, used large quantities of water and required a number of pits. A series of post-medieval tan pits were discovered during the 1970s excavations near St. Peter's church, Northampton. Following the development of tanning by chromium salts in rotating drums, the process was introduced in Northampton in 1898. The process took over from pit tanning, and was concentrated in the towns. All tanneries have now closed and most of the buildings have been demolished.

3

The timber in the former extensively wooded areas of the county had many uses, including ship-building. Reducing the trees to useable wood was by hand-sawing until the mid-19thC after which steam engine-driven sawing, and later, planing machinery came into general use. The activity tended to move from the country to the towns, especially when imported timber was brought in. Little remains of these once extensive town saw-mills.

Textiles

Until the early 19thC, the woollen industry was important in Northamptonshire, as in many other counties. It was mainly a domestic activity but the final stage of fulling was carried out in water-powered fulling mills. There were at least 15 fulling mills in the county. Some of these survive although they were subsequently used for other purposes, for example paper-making. There are records of at least nine paper mills in Northamptonshire including Rush Mills on the River Nene at Hardingstone, which made the paper for the first Penny Black postage stamps. Another first in the county was the first water-powered cotton mill in the world which operated at Northampton from 1742 until 1761.

The county's clothing industry developed during the latter part of the 19thC, centred in North-ampton, Kettering and Wellingborough. Although this industry has declined, some imposing factory buildings remain. Several clothing firms established branch factories in nearby villages and interesting examples are at Brigstock and Cottingham.

Boots & shoes

Although footwear production in England was generally regarded as a craft industry in med-ieval times, there is some evidence of large scale production. Northampton's first recorded large order for footwear was in 1642 for the army and this may have been the impetus for the subsequent development of the industry in the county. During the 18thC, it became established in Daventry, Kettering and Welling-borough, then Higham Ferrers, Rushden and Raunds before spreading to their surrounding villages. Initially shoemaking was entirely a hand process, with most of the work done at the

Mounts shoe factory, Overstone Road, Northampton in 1965

workers' homes, leading in some places to separate outworkers' workshops at each house. The manufacturer usually had little more than a warehouse from which work was issued out and taken in. Changes came in the latter part of the 19thC with the increasing use of powered machinery and production carried out almost entirely in factories. Despite the marked decline in the industry during the second half of the 20thC, many of the factory buildings remain, often adapted for other purposes. Some are of considerable architectural interest.

Engineering

Engineering developed from two main sources. One was in connection with improvements in farm machinery, where blacksmiths and wheelwrights evolved into agricultural engineers and then general engineers. The other source was the introduction and development of machinery for making boots and shoes, where small firms changed from repairing machines to making them and then diversifying to manufacture equipment for other industries. As the necessary skills became available in all the county's towns, other engineering businesses developed or transferred from elsewhere. One example was the fore-runner of The Express Lift Company in Northamp-ton where the tall lift testing tower is a reminder of this now demolished engineering works.

Brewing

From the beginning of the 19thC, 'common' (i.e. commercial) brewers began to dominate brewing, taking over from the domestic brewers and brewing victuallers (i.e. publicans). A few examples of the remains of the brewhouses used by the latter still survive in the county, as at Naseby. The main growth of the common brewers was in larger towns and Northampton became a significant brewing centre. In 1900 there were 6 breweries operating in the town. More surprisingly, Oundle also had a considerable brewing industry with 3 breweries and substantial buildings remain of two of these.

NBC Brewery, Bridge Street, Northampton in 1967

Distribution

In medieval times, distribution of goods from producer to consumer was achieved through markets and fairs held in open spaces. Later, market halls provided cover, whilst permanent cattle markets proved better facilities for both animals and commerce. Buying directly from a producer's premises was supplemented - and eventually supplanted - by retailers, each selling goods from a number of different producers. These developments in retailing led to the rise of wholesale merchants who often had impressive buildings, for example the range of Co-operative Wholesale Society warehouses of different dates in Northampton.

Transport

Northamptonshire's long narrow shape on a south-west to north-east axis ensured that whatever the form of transport, major routes from London to the Midlands and the North passed through it. During the 18thC and early 19thC, a number of turnpike roads were established in the county, accompanied by the construction of toll-houses and the erection of milestones. Sadly many of these have been removed but the toll-houses at Staverton and Weedon have been converted to other uses and there are good examples of the London to Holyhead road milestones at Daventry.

The River Nene was made navigable up to Northampton in 1761 following a number of improvements including the building of locks which bypassed the weirs for the numerous mills on the river. The first canal in the county was the Oxford Canal, opened from near Coventry to Banbury in 1778. The main-line of the Grand Junction Canal opened in 1805 after the completion of Blisworth tunnel. During its construction, from 1800 a railed way of flanged plates was laid over Blisworth Hill, linking the completed sections of the canal north of Blisworth and south of Stoke Bruerne. Excavations on its route in 1969 revealed four rows of stone blocks. On completion of the tunnel, parts of the railed way were incorporated in the 'railroad' which ran from the canal at Blisworth to Northampton until 1815 when the branch canal was opened to the town, making a connection with the River Nene. The line from the Grand Junction Canal (now called the Grand Union) at Norton Junction towards Leicester was completed in 1814, having a very circuitous course on the summit level. Apart from the branch to Buckingham from Cosgrove, all of the county's canals remain open and the tow-paths provide easy access to the interesting features along them.

The first main-line railway through Northamptonshire was the London and Birmingham Railway which opened throughout in 1838, later taken over by the London & North Western Railway

5

and forming today's West Coast Main Line. The Great Western Railway's line from Oxford to Banbury (later part of the Great Western's main-line to Birmingham), barely touching North-amptonshire, was opened in 1850. The Midland Railway's extension from Leicester to Hitchin and later direct to London opened in 1857, passing through Kettering and Wellingborough, forming the modern Midland Main Line. Northampton did not become a railway centre of any importance until the completion of the Roade-Northampton-Rugby line in 1882. The Great Central Railway's extension to London opened in 1898, turning the village of Woodford Halse into a railway town. Together with branches and cross-country lines, these provided the county with over 90 stations. Following the closure of many lines, mainly during the 1950s and 1960s, there are now only six stations open but many features of past railways remain.

Services
Along with developments in manufacturing and transport there came improvements in living standards. This was not only in housing but also in the provision of public services such as water supply, waste disposal, illumination and, later, power. A waterworks was set up at Nunn Mills in 1722 to supply nearby Northampton but abandoned by 1754. The Northampton Waterworks was established in 1837 with a pumping station in Cliftonville. With the continual increase in their populations during the latter part of the 19thC, the county's towns had to go beyond their boundaries to construct reservoirs and pumping stations. These are still significant features at Cransley, Ravensthorpe and Sywell.

Northampton gasworks started in 1824 and was followed by works in all the county's towns and some of the larger villages. Many of the smaller concerns were acquired by the large town-based companies but first nationalisation and then the change to North Sea gas caused the closure of all the county's gasworks.

In 1891 the Northampton Electric Light and Power Company commenced supply from its Angel Lane generating station. Kettering, Rushden and Wellingborough soon had their own generating stations. In 1919 NELPCo. commenced supply from its Hardingstone Junction generating station, and then began to take over other Northamptonshire companies. Hardingstone Junction closed in the late 1970s and the two cooling towers were demolished soon afterwards.

Although the provision of water, gas and electricity supply is usually associated with urban utilit-ies, the owners of country estates, such as Castle Ashby, made their own provision for these services.

Entertainment
Life was also improved by the increased opportunities for activities outside the workplace. Mechanics Institutes, band clubs, sporting and other societies did not usually require special buildings unlike the entertain-ment industry. Changing public tastes and commercial press-ures have discarded many earlier commercial enterprises but there is still evidence of early theatres, cinemas and other facilities in the county.

Playground equipment in Wicksteed Park Kettering manufactured by Wicksteed Engineering in the mid 20thC

INTRODUCTION TO THE 2ND EDITION

In the ten years or so that have elapsed since the 1st Edition was prepared there have inevitably been changes. Some sites have been destroyed by fire, others demolished at the behest of a land developer, in at least one case without permission of the relevant district council (the former maltings on St Peter's Way in Northampton). Others have been saved after much public outcry, notably the former Express Lift Tower at Northampton, now once again testing lifts.

Some sites in the first edition have been modified or changed in such a way that the features for which they were originally included are no longer present, or in some cases a more pertinent example has come to light. Finally, it has been necessary to update entries to take account of changes of use, accessibility and to correct one or two errors that crept into the first edition.

KEY TO GAZETTEER

Sites are listed by town or civil parish in alphabetical order. Within Northampton, they are listed by geographical area and in a logical route order within each area. In other towns and larger conurbations, sites are listed in roughly a clockwise direction starting from north. Entries are listed by type in the Index – on pages 96 and 97.

The reference next to the parish name can be used to identify its location on the county map on pages 8 and 9. Separate maps in the Gazetteer show the approximate location of sites in Braunston, Kettering, Northampton, Rushden and Wellingborough.

Key to symbols etc.

Abbreviations
LNWR   London & North Western Railway
WW1 or WW2   World War One or Two
18thC   18th Century (and similar for other centuries)

Access to site
O   Site open to the public, often with visitor facilities. Be sure to ascertain opening hours before visiting. Where appropriate, a website or telephone number is given.

★   Site can be viewed from a public road or footpath or other public route through or near the site. This does not imply permission to wander anywhere at will.

❑   Site is on private property and permission must be sought for access.

Protected status
LBI   Listed Grade I
LBII*   Listed Grade II*
LBII   Listed Grade II
C   Within a Conservation Area
S   Scheduled Ancient Monument

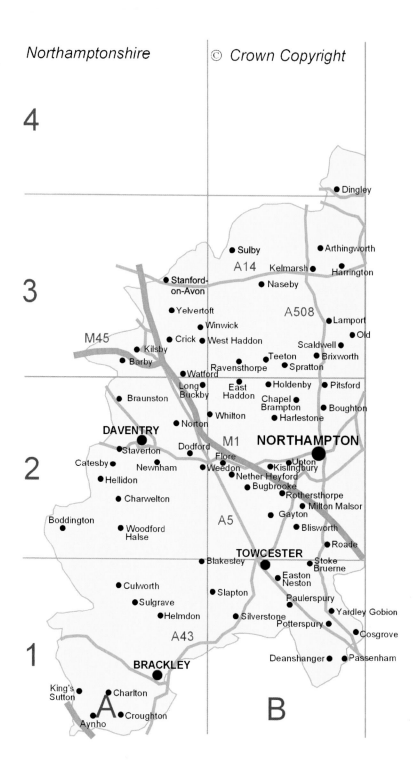

Northamptonshire © Crown Copyright

4

3

● Dingley

● Sulby   ● Arthingworth
A14 Kelmarsh ●   ●
● Stanford-   Harrington
on-Avon   ● Naseby

● Yelvertoft   A508
● Winwick   ● Lamport
M45   ● Crick ● West Haddon   Scaldwell ● ● Old
● Kilsby   ● Teeton ● Brixworth
● Barby   Ravensthorpe ● Spratton
● Watford
Long ● East   ● Holdenby ● Pitsford
● Braunston Buckby Haddon Chapel ●
Brampton   ● Boughton
● Whilton   ● Harlestone
● Norton
DAVENTRY
● Dodford M1 NORTHAMPTON
● Staverton
Catesby ●   Flore   ● Upton
● Newnham ● Weedon ● Kislingbury
● Hellidon   ● Nether Heyford
● Bugbrooke
● Charwelton   ● Rothersthorpe
● Milton Malsor
Boddington ● Gayton
● ● Woodford A5   ● Blisworth
Halse
● Roade
TOWCESTER
● Blakesley   ● Stoke
Bruerne
● Culworth   Easton
Neston
● Sulgrave ● Slapton Paulerspury ●
● Helmdon ● Silverstone   ● Yardley Gobion
Potterspury ●
A43   ● Cosgrove

King's ●   ● Deanshanger ● Passenham
BRACKLEY
King's ●
Sutton ● Charlton
A ● Croughton
Aynho   B

2

1

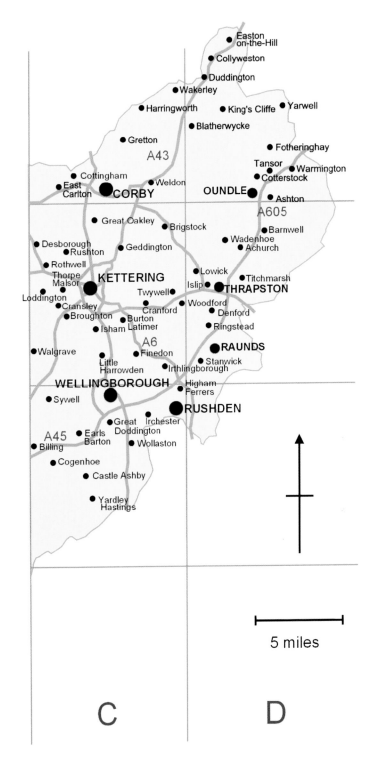

5 miles

C   D

9

ACHURCH   D3

I Water pump
TL 024829 ★ LBII
On the east side of the Lilford to Thorpe
Waterville road, opposite a row of former
Lilford estate workers' cottages is a well and
pump built as a memorial to Thomas Athurton
Powys in 1882. The single-throw pump was
worked by a five-spoked wheel, of which only
the stumps of the spokes remain, on a crank-
shaft supported by two wooden A-frames.
The whole is surmounted by a narrow, tiled
roof carried on elaborate brackets from two
uprights, each with a carved angel, all in wood.
The well was in use until 1950 when the
village was connected to mains water.

ARTHINGWORTH   B3

2 Underground fuel distribution depot
SP 746806 ★
On the east side of the Brampton Valley Way
¼ mile north of the Kelmarsh to Arthingworth road. It is a relic of aviation fuel
distribution during WW2 undertaken by the
Petroleum Board (a consortium of major oil
companies). This was a key depot with rail
access from the adjacent LNWR's Northampton to Market Harborough line.

ASHTON   D4

3 Former watermill
TL 052882 ★ LBII C
On a loop of the River Nene, alongside the
road from Polebrook to the north end of
Oundle. Ashton Mill is a 3-storey brick building with a Collyweston slate roof. Originally a
corn mill, it was converted in 1900 by the
Rothschild family to supply direct current
electricity to the newly built mansion and farm
at Ashton Wold, as well as piped drinking
water to the water tower there (see Site 4)
and to the village of Ashton. The original two
Gilks water turbines, two 1937 Blackstone oil
engines (replacing the original Crossley
engine), overhead shafting, pumps and
electrical equipment remain in-situ. The mill
was part of the National Dragonfly Museum
housed in adjacent buildings, but this has now
closed and the mill is derelict.

4 Former water tower
TL 078881 ❑ LBII
On the Ashton Wold estate, north-west of
Ashton Wold House, 1½ miles east of Ashton
village green and 2½ miles east of Oundle.
The water tower was built of stone c1900 in a
vernacular revival style and is reminiscent of
an Italian renaissance castle. It consists of a 3-
storey section with a Collyweston slate
hipped roof, louvred vents and pseudo
machicolation, plus a larger 2-storey section
with flat roof and crenellated parapets. Water
tanks occupied both sections at first floor
level, the water having been pumped from
Ashton Mill (see Site 3). Planning permission
has been given to convert the water tower to
a residence.

4 Former water tower, Ashton

5 Milepost
TL 050894 ★ LBII
Situated in the verge on the west side of the
Oundle to Peterborough road, just north of
the turn to Cotterstock. Of stone, it is about
10½in (25cm) square and 20in (50cm) high.
On the face towards the road near ground
level is the inscription: *12 miles to Peterborough.* There are very worn inscriptions on
the adjacent sides.

AYNHO   A1
6 Canal bridge and weir
SP 498323 ★ LBII

The B4031 Aynho to Deddington road crosses the Oxford Canal by a stone bridge (No.190). This has a more shallow curve than is usual on canals. North of the road and by the side of the tow-path on the west of the canal, is a semi-circular weir for the overflow from the canal.

7 Former canal wharf
SP 498324 ★

On the east side of the Oxford Canal, a little north of the B4031 Aynho to Deddington road bridge. The site of an extensive wharf opened in 1788, which was used to unload house-coal and stone from the Midlands and salt from Cheshire. It was also an outlet for local agricultural products such as hay, straw and corn. Although much altered, one of the several warehouses that served the wharf still survives, and can be seen with its roof overhanging the canal amidst the more recent marina development.

7 Former canal wharf, Aynho

8 Canal weir lock
SP 494337 ★

Reached by walking south for about ¼ mile along the tow-path from the B4100 road bridge over the Oxford Canal. Just after the accommodation bridge (No.188 - LBII) is a shallow lock (No.33) of unusual construction. Its primary purpose was to protect the Oxford Canal from any surge in the River

Cherwell, which crosses the canal at the same level on the other side of the bridge. Soon after it was built in 1790, it was enlarged to its present lozenge-shape, with a breadth of about 20ft (6m) at the widest point, compensating for its very small fall - less than 1ft (30cm). This alteration ensures that when this lock is emptied, sufficient water passes into the canal to fill the next down-hill lock, which is Somerton Deep Lock with a 12ft (3.6m) fall, two miles further south.

9 Former Aynho station
SP 498324 ★

On the north side of the B4031 Aynho to Deddington road. A single-storey stone building with low-pitched roof built to Brunel's design for small stations. Opened in 1850 on the Great Western Railway's broad-gauge line between Oxford and Banbury. The station closed in 1964 and platforms were removed. No public access to interior but exterior can be seen from the B4031 road bridge and the former station yard.

10 Former Aynho Park Platform
SP 500324 ★

On the south side of the B4031 Aynho to Deddington road. A typical Great Western Railway brick-built station entrance building remains in derelict condition at road level on the railway line between Ashendon, north of Princes Risborough (on the Great Central and Great Western joint line) and a junction with the Oxford to Birmingham line about ¾ mile north of Aynho station. The line opened in 1910 to provide a direct Paddington to Birmingham route. The 'station' closed in 1963.

11 Railway flyover
SP 497328 ❑

Approximately ½ mile north of the B4031 between Aynho and Deddington. The acutely skewed 10-bay Warren girder bridge of riveted steel construction on blue brick abutments was built in 1910. It carries the single 'down' (northbound) track of the line from Ashendon (Princes Risborough) to Aynho over the Oxford to Banbury line, with which it makes a junction about ½ mile north.

14 Former offices for Pearce's tannery, Billing

BARBY A3

12 Former windmill
SP 541696 ★ LBII

Situated west of the crossroads, south of the village. The brick shell of a three-storey tower corn mill, about 30ft (9m) high and 24ft (8m) diameter at the base. Built about 1830 to replace an earlier post mill, the sails were blown off in the 1870s. Milling continued until the early 1900s using a steam engine housed in a separate building (demolished in the late 1970s) adjacent to the mill. About 1997 work started to restore the tower; the cap has been reconstructed and the mill is now a dwelling.

BARNWELL D3

13 Former watermill
TL 038868 ★ LBII

On the west side of a lock on the navigable stream of the River Nene, close to the road entering the south side of Oundle from the A605. Confusingly now called *Oundle Mill*, the former Barnwell watermill is an impressive three-storey stone building with stone slate roof and a large wooden lucam. In 1893 the horizontal mill-stones were replaced by a roller milling plant, powered by a Vortex-type water turbine but the large internal undershot water-wheel was still there in 1939 by which time the mill was no longer at work. The Buccleuch Estates sold the mill in the late 1960s and it is now a bar and restaurant. From the latter, one can look down onto the original wheel race under the mill.

BILLING C2

14 Former W Pearce & Co. tannery
SP 802627 ★ LBII

On the south side of the A4500 Wellingborough Rd in Great Billing, ½ mile east of the interchange with A43 Lumbertubs Way. The tannery of W Pearce & Co. opened in 1939; the office building is notable for its art-deco style with white rendering and glazed tile embellishment. The tannery closed in 2001 and the site is due to be converted to housing but the office block will remain.

15 Former watermill
SP 814611 ★

On a loop from the River Nene, Billing Mill is west of the Billing to Brafield road, south of the Nene Valley Way (A45). In 1274 there was a fulling mill on the site. The present three-storey stone corn mill with slate roof is joined at its south end by the two-storey brick former mill cottage. The buildings dating from the early 19thC, were adapted for a Museum of Milling in 1968 and in the mid-1990s converted into a restaurant and bar, retaining the iron Poncelet-type undershot water-wheel and some machinery but now all behind glass.

16 Miniature railway
SP 809615 ○

West of the Billing to Brafield road, just south of its junction with the Nene Valley Way (A45). Billing Aquadrome is on the site of a large gravel extraction enterprise which dates from the 1930s. It had a 2ft (60cm) gauge tramway which in part was later used as a pleasure railway for the users of the Aquadrome. In 2010 a new 15in (38cm) gauge track was laid to run a steam outline, diesel-hauled train. (www.billingaquadrome.com)

17 Commemorative stone
SP 804607 ★
Situated on the south side of Clifford Hill Lock on the River Nene is a stone commemorating the financing of the construction of the lock by the Hon. Spencer Compton one of the candidates for Northampton in the parliamentary elections of 1761.

BLAKESLEY A1

18 Former windmill
SP 623504 ★ LBII
Situated at Quinbury End, just off the west side of Maidford road. Built of brick in 1832 as a six-storey tower corn mill, carrying a domed cap, four sails and a fantail, it ceased work in the 1890s. Soon after it was reduced by 20ft (6m) to its present height, all machinery removed and used as a builder's store. It has been converted to a dwelling and a shallow curved cap has been placed on top of the tower.

BLATHERWYCKE D4

19 Former watermill
SP 980967 ★ LBII
On the south side of the road between Blatherwycke and King's Cliffe. This stone building, a corn mill, might be considered to be the most architecturally interesting of the surviving mills in the county. The east (downstream) side is of three-storeys with industrial-style windows, whilst the west side is of two-storeys with Gothic windows. Stewarts & Lloyds Ltd. acquired the mill in the 1930s and electric pumps were installed to take water from the lake to their new integrated iron, steel and tube works being developed at Corby.

The mill is private property and the machinery has been removed but there are excellent views of the exterior from the road.

BLISWORTH B2

Blisworth was in a key location for industrial developments in the late 18thC and early 19thC. The Grand Junction Canal Company built the canal (now called the Grand Union) from London to Braunston via Blisworth and also constructed the earliest tramway in the county to transport goods over Blisworth Hill whilst the canal tunnel was being completed. In 1838 the London & Birmingham Railway also passed through Blisworth which later became the junction for lines to Northampton, Stratford-on-Avon and Banbury. Both limestone and ironstone were extensively quarried in the vicinity of the village which is notable for having the earliest (c1820) limestone quarry tramway in the county (see Site 20). It also boasted one of the earliest ironstone tramways in the county – from the Stoke Rd allotments down to the canal in c1852 – but little sign of this now remains.

20 Former stoneworks
SP 730529 ★ LBII
On the east side of Stoke Rd, near the north entrance to Blisworth canal tunnel (Site 26), ½ mile south of the village centre. A range of stone buildings, now part of a farm, formed the stoneworks which operated from the 1820s to c1912. The house fronting onto the road is of classical style with *Blisworth Stone Works* inscribed beneath the central pediment. Little remains of the former limestone

19 Former watermill, Blatherwycke

quarry which extended to the east of the road and utilised a tramway to carry stone down to the canal at Blisworth.

21 Former steam mill
SP 724534 ★ LBII C

Situated to the west of the canal on the north side of the road from the village which heads south-west to the A43. This large brick building of five-storeys, eight bays alongside the canal and eight bays across the northern gable ends, was built in 1879 for Joseph Westley & Sons (who also operated Nunn Mills, near Northampton). The steam engine was housed in the two-storey building across the three northern bays on the west side of the mill. In 1920 the mill was purchased by the Northampton Cooperative Society who sold it in about 1928. Subsequently it was used as a warehouse by various firms until the 1970s. The building is now converted to apartments.

21 Former steam mill, Blisworth

22 Railway bridge over road
SP 728541 ★ LBII

About ½ mile north of Blisworth on the road to Milton Malsor. This is a fine bridge with a semi-circular arch of dressed stone some 30ft (9m) high at the crown. It was constructed by Richard Dunkley of Blisworth to carry the London & Birmingham Railway over the Cotton End to Towcester turnpike road. Opened in 1838, the bridge still carries West Coast Main Line trains. On the embankment to the south-west of the bridge the first Blisworth station was sited. North-east of the bridge is

a terrace of 12 early railway (probably London & Birmingham Railway) cottages.

23 Canal junction
SP 720550 ★

Just north of Grand Union Canal bridge No.48 for the Rothersthorpe to Tiffield road. Gayton Junction is where the heavily-locked 5-mile long branch canal to the River Nene in Northampton begins. It opened in 1815, with a total of 17 locks falling over 100ft (30m), replacing a horse-worked railed way which was used from 1805. Note the cast-iron milepost (LBII) on the northern corner of the junction, inscribed: *GJCCo / Braunston 16¾ miles / Northampton 5 miles*.

24 Railway bridge over canal
SP 723544 ★

About ½ mile north-west of Blisworth village, reached via the tow-path alongside the Grand Union Canal some 200yds north of Blisworth Station Road. Beneath - and encased in - the modern concrete bridge which carries the West Coast Main Line over the canal, can be seen the wrought-iron framework of the original bridge built by the London & Birmingham Railway in the late 1830s.

25 Canal tow-path edging
SP 724534 ★ C

Immediately south of bridge No.51, which takes the road to Towcester over the Grand Union Canal. The tow-path is edged at the canal side by stone blocks, originally used as sleeper blocks on the London & Birmingham Railway when it opened in 1838. In each block there is a rectangular recess situated diagonally, with a central hole for securing the rail.

26 Blisworth canal tunnel entrance
SP 729529 ★

A path heading west from Stoke Rd, opposite *The Stoneworks* (Site 20) at the south end of the village, descends to the tow-path in the cutting. This leads to the north entrance of the 1¾ mile long Blisworth canal tunnel which eventually opened on March 25th 1805. This brick-lined tunnel is wide enough for two 7ft (2.1m) wide boats to pass but there is no tow-path, so the canal horses had to walk over the hill. In the early days, boats were propelled through by boat-men pushing on poles against wooden chocks, set at 9ft (2.7m) intervals on guide rails fixed to the tunnel walls. From 1827, the canal company provided professional leggers who lay on boards rigged out from the boat and used their feet to walk the walls inside the tunnel. The leggers were replaced by steam tugs in 1871. In 1903 the canal had to be drained to allow the north portal to be completely re-built and repairs made to the brick-work inside which was regularly collapsing in places. To the west of the Blisworth to Stoke Bruerne road, along the line of the tunnel, large mounds of earth which had been winched up through vertical shafts during construction, can still be seen in places. Most of these shafts were filled in, but following the introduction of steam-powered boats, a number were re-opened in the 1860s to help with ventilation. Small round brick towers mark some of the shafts in use today. The deepest of these is over 140ft (42m) from ground level to the canal bed. (See also Site 376)

26 North portal Blisworth Tunnel

27 Route of former tramroad
SP 724533 - 729528 ★
The Blisworth Hill Railway connected the canal at Stoke Bruerne bottom lock with the canal at Blisworth, from 1800 until 1805 when Blisworth Tunnel was completed. On the west side of the canal the route can be distinguish-ed by a path between property boundaries

and the edge of the canal. In the fields the route is denoted by a level width of ground with a fairly constant gradient up the hill, cutting across the natural contours of the land. Two cast-iron markers bearing the initials *GJCCo* (Grand Junction Canal Company) delineate the canal company's property in the vicinity of the tramroad. In the field above the north entrance to the tunnel (SP 729528) is an embankment for the tramroad. (See also Site 377)

28 Milepost
SP 717528 ★
On the south-east side of the Blisworth to Towcester road (formerly the A43), by an isolated group of houses just over ½ mile south of the canal crossing. An original milestone of the Northampton to Towcester turnpike dating from 1794-5. When the stone was re-erected about 1993 it was a little distance from its original position and the new cast-iron plate is not an accurate replica of the original.

BODDINGTON   A2
29 Canal reservoir
SP 493534 & SP 498532 ★
There are 2 car parks at the north end of the reservoir, which lies south of the Byfield to Upper Boddington road. The dam for the reservoir is at its south end. The original reservoir was completed in 1811 and provided water for the summit level of the Oxford Canal at a point 2½ miles to the west by a winding feeder channel. It was enlarged in 1833 and the dam rebuilt in 1983.

BOUGHTON   B2
30 Former watermill
SP 737657 ★
On the Nene North Water about ¼ mile north of the bridge for the A5199 Northampton to Chapel Brampton road. A large stone-built mill of three storeys, it changed from corn grinding to paper making before 1717 but by 1835 it was working again as a corn mill with three pairs of stones. The water-wheel and machinery were taken out in the

1950s and the mill is now part of a riding school.

BRACKLEY   A1

31 Former watermill
SP 595372 ★

Situated at the end of Mill Lane, running north from Buckingham Road, on the north side of a builders merchant's yard. A former corn mill, now a three-storey stone building with a slate ridged roof, in earlier years the roof was of thatch. The mill has been gutted of all machinery and has been converted to residential accommodation. Adjoining on the west side is the former mill house of two storeys.

32 Former fire station
SP 587372 ★ C

On the east side of the High Street, just south of the National Trust Park. The 1887 Fire Engine House is a single-storey stone building and has a slate ridged roof with the gable end-on to High Street. This is surmounted by a small brick arch with the words *Fire Bell* carved in stone - but no bell! Behind is a brick hose tower with louvred openings in the top storey, and a slate ridged roof. The building is empty its future undecided.

33 Former Brackley (GC) station
SP 590380 ★

Approx. ½ mile north-east of the market place on Top Station Rd off the south-east side of Northampton Rd. Opened in 1899 on the Great Central Railway, only the station building remains, now an auto spares company. The island platform was reached from the station building via a footbridge, now gone. The station closed in 1966.

34 Former goods shed
SP 590378 ★

In what is now an industrial estate on Top Station Rd accessed down behind the former station building (Site 33). The former Great Central Railway goods shed, built of brick and still retaining its projecting canopy, was in use from 1899 to 1966. It is converted to offices with the erroneous name - *The Engine Shed*.

34 Former goods shed, Brackley

BRAUNSTON   A2

The Oxford Canal was built to carry coal from the Midlands to the navigable River Thames at Oxford. It opened as far as Banbury in 1778 and was completed to Oxford in 1790. It was joined at Braunston in 1796, by the Grand Junction Canal, (now known as the Grand Union) built with wide locks to provide a much faster passage to the tidal Thames at Brentford. The latter opened as far as Weedon in June 1796 but there was no through route to London this way until 1805. In 1834, works to considerably reduce the distance of the winding Oxford Canal included a major diversion at Braunston. Three miles of the canal were abandoned and a new junction created about ½ mile west of the original. The various features are shown in Sites 35-48.

35 Former course of canal
SP 535655 - 533645 ★

In the fields to the south-west of the A428 opposite the entrance to the marina and south of the embankment for the former LNWR's Daventry to Leamington line. The sinuous pre-1834 course of the Oxford Canal shows as a distinct depression in the ground as it follows the contour to cross the River Leam, some stretches still in water.

36 Canal aqueduct
SP 529657 ★ LBII C

On the Oxford Canal, ¼ mile south-west of its 'new' junction with the Grand Union Canal, the canal is carried over the River Leam (the county boundary) by three brick arches. The

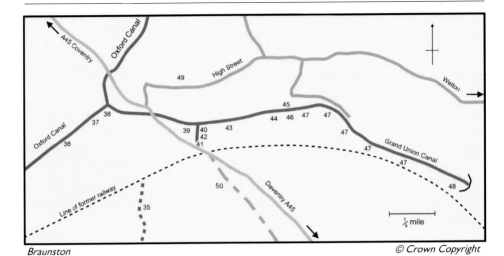

Braunston

centre one is over the river itself whilst the flanking arches provide access to the fields either side of the canal embankment.

37 Combined accommodation and turnover canal bridge
SP 531659 ★ LBII C
On the Oxford Canal, close to its 'new' junction with the Grand Union Canal. The north-east part of the bridge has curved inclines from the tow-paths on each side of the canal. This enabled boats working on the London to Birmingham route to pass under without unhitching the rope from the horse. The south-west part of the bridge connects fields on each side of the canal, a brick wall across the bridge preventing access to the tow-paths.

38 Canal junction
SP 532660 ★ C
Between the two bridges for the A45 road over the original line of the Oxford Canal. The 'new' line of 1834 heads south-west from a two-branch junction, through twin cast-iron arched roving bridges (Nos. 93 and 94 - LBII), with a brick-built link having an arch standing on the island formed by the junction.

39 Former canal toll-house
SP 538658 ★ LBII C
Adjacent to the southern bank of the canal approximately ¼ mile east of the southern

A45 road bridge crossing is the two-storey red brick building with a hipped slate roof, now known as the *Stop House* after its refurbishment in 1990. It dates from the opening of the junction of the Grand Junction Canal with the original route of the Oxford Canal and is now the British Waterways Regional Office, together with an information and exhibition room. Under the vegetation on the north bank opposite the former toll-house, can be seen evidence of the Oxford Canal Company's stop lock, built here in 1834. It was a narrow lock with a few inches fall, which enabled boats to be easily gauged to find out the weight of their cargo, so that the toll due could be calculated. The stop lock was removed and the toll-house taken out of use in 1931, as part of a plan to widen the route to Birmingham. The brickwork of the lock chamber north wall, with its coping is still in place, and the recesses where the gateposts stood and the slots for the paddle gear rods are visible from across the canal.

40 Former canal junction
SP 538659 ★ C
A few yards east along the canal bank from the toll-house, the main entrance to the marina is part of the original line of the Oxford Canal. The junction was widened in 1816, when the Grand Junction Canal Co. built their short narrow Braunston Branch Canal from

here, in a south-east direction, around the side of their reservoir, to serve a large warehouse built near the Daventry Road. Part of this branch has been filled in and the rest incorporated into the marina complex that occupies the site today. The point where the branch left the main-line junction can be clearly seen from the cast-iron roving bridge (LBII) over the Oxford Canal. The latter was probably erected by the Grand Junction Canal Co. some time after the branch was built. In 1834, when the diversion was built, three miles of the original line of the canal south of the junction were abandoned leaving a short arm here as far as the present A45 road.

41 Canal dry docks
SP 539658 ★ LBII C
At the south end of the truncated old line of canal are two covered dry docks. Part of the wharf was leased from the Oxford Canal by Fellows, Morton and Clayton who built a new dock in 1901 and another, dated 1909, across the former main-line near its end. The older one has a hipped roof over very low walls. Both docks were for steam boats and originally had lantern roofs to allow fumes to escape. After FMC closed in Braunston in 1934, these docks were used by Nursers (the renowned boat-building family) for painting and repairing. Despite having new owners from 1941 the yard continued to be known as Nursers until the late 1960s.

42 Former boat building shed
SP 539658 ★ LBII C
Alongside the east side of the old line of the Oxford Canal. The long building with roof overhanging the canal was used for building boats by Nursers. Boats were launched sideways into the canal.

43 Former canal reservoirs
SP 539658 - 543659 ★ C
To the south of the tow-path, east of the main entrance to the marina, is a series of reservoirs built by the Grand Junction Canal Co. from 1806 and originally connected by a siphon. The bottom lock of the Braunston flight was emptied by boat-men lifting paddles

to let the water pass into these reservoirs, instead of being lost to the Company by flowing into the Oxford Canal at the junction. The water was held in the reservoirs until it was required again in the summit pound. It was back-pumped into a leat running along the hillside to the top of the flight, where it replaced water used to work the locks at both ends of this 4-mile long summit pound. These reservoirs are now incorporated into the modern marina complex. Some hundred yards east of the junction, access has been made to the reservoirs from the main-line canal, and a footbridge salvaged from the Buckingham Branch in 1962, takes the tow-path across the water connection.

44 Pumping engine house
SP 544659 ★ C
Just west of bridge No.2 at Little Braunston, and on the south side of the canal. A red brick building with a slate roof and a square-section chimney, lettered vertically *GJCC* in lighter coloured brick. Built in 1896 to house steam driven centrifugal pumps, this replaced the earlier engine house of c1805 for beam engines, situated some distance to the south. The pumps took water from below the bottom lock up to the summit level of the canal through Braunston tunnel. The steam engine was replaced by a diesel engine in 1940 and electric pumps replaced this in 1958.

45 Former gauging dock
SP 544659 ★ LBII C
East of bridge No.2 by the bottom lock (No.1). The long low brick building with a slate roof standing on the north side of the

45 Former gauging dock, Braunston

canal covers a special dock built in 1816. This was one of the canal company's two gauging stations where individual boats were calibrated, This involved measuring the depth to which a boat would sink, when loaded with a range of weights. Calibration records were distributed to canal company toll-houses, to allow the correct toll to be determined from the depth of the boat in the water, without emptying the cargo from the boat.

46 Canal cottages
SP 545659 ★ LBII C
The row of cottages on the south side of bottom lock (No.1) was built for canal workers in the late 18thC.

47 Flight of canal locks
SP 545660 - 553656 ★ C
The flight of 6 wide locks (Nos.1-6) in just over ½ mile raises the canal a total of 35ft 6in (10.8m) to the summit level (lock Nos. 1 and 3 are LBII). Over this length the canal is crossed by three bridges (Nos.3-5) and alongside lock No.3 there is a canalside pub, the *Admiral Nelson*, converted from a farmhouse which started selling beer to the navigators building the canal and then to the boatmen. It was much altered during the 1980s.

48 Braunston canal tunnel entrance
SP 557654 ★ LBII C
Reached by the tow-path heading east from the top lock of the Braunston flight or by taking the footpath from the Daventry end of the tunnel. Opened in 1796 the tunnel, lined with locally produced bricks, is 2042yds (1867m) long, wide enough for two 7ft (2.1m) beam boats to pass but has no tow-path. There are three circular brick airshafts, all by the footpath over the hill which follows the route the horses would have taken whilst the boats were legged through the tunnel. Legging was replaced by steam-tugs in 1871.

49 Former windmill
SP 537661 ★ LBII
Standing just east of the church on the north side of the road into the village from the A45. Built in 1800 for milling corn, it is of red brick,

and was originally eight storeys high. This tower mill had a conical cap carrying four sails, which drove three pairs of stones and two dressing machines. Milling ceased in the 1890s. About 1910, the sails, cap and machinery were removed and the height reduced by one storey. After being used as a store for many years, in the 1970s a dome roof, originally made for a grain silo, was fitted and the mill converted to a residence.

49 Former windmill, Braunston

50 Original route of Holyhead Road
SP 540656 ★
This part of the former route is now called Old Road and heads uphill in a south-east direction from the A45 at the south end of Braunston village. The gradient for horse-drawn traffic is quite daunting. Today's single-track remnant is tarmacadam for the first 400yds or so, serving some 18thC and 19thC cottages, then deteriorates into a farm track.

BRIGSTOCK   C3
51 Former Wallis clothing factory
SP 944856 ★ LBII
Off High St at the junction of Back Lane and Old Dry Lane at the north-west edge of the village. This imposing 4-storey factory was

constructed of stone in 1873 for Frederic Wallis as a clothing factory, later becoming part of Wallis & Linnell which operated until 1979. Note the narrowness of the building compared to its length, so as to maximise illumination from the round-headed iron-framed windows. Now converted to offices. (Compare with the Wallis factory at Cottingham - Site 81.)

51 Former Wallis clothing factory, Brigstock

52 Former watermill
SP 945854 ☐ LBII C
In the village on Harper's Brook, just south-west of the Mill Lane/Latham Street corner. A 3-storey stone building with slate roof having negligible eaves giving a very bulky appearance to the mill. The 21ft 6in (6.6m) diameter breast-shot iron water-wheel is outside the west end of the building in which some machinery remains. By 1914 steam power had been introduced. Originally a corn mill and now converted to a dwelling.

53 Former water tower & pump house
SP 959869 ★
The buildings are situated a short distance east of the road to Lower Benefield almost opposite Fermyn Woods Hall for which they provided the water supply. A Ruston Hornsby oil engine powered a line-shaft from which belts drove reciprocating pumps. This plant was in the north-east part of the long single-storey stone building with a hipped slate roof. Attached to the north-west side of the pump house is a 40ft (12m) high stone water tower surmounted by a pyramidal slate roof. The pumping plant was removed and the buildings converted to a dwelling in about 1995.

BRIXWORTH   B3
54 Former fire engine house
SP 747711 ★ C
On Cross Hill is a single-storey stone building with brick quoins and a round entrance arch, now blocked in with stones. It was built in 1912, the village's first purpose-built fire station, housing a horse-drawn appliance. This slate roofed building with brick dentillation at the eaves is now incorporated into a dwelling.

BROUGHTON   C3
55 Blacksmith's forge
SP 834759 ★
On the east side of the road to Cransley is the two-storey brick-built forge where the James family have been in business since the 1840s. It has developed from traditional blacksmiths' work to high quality restoration work using a variety of techniques.

BUGBROOKE   B2
56 Former watermill
SP 679588 ☐
On the River Nene, at the end of a private road running north from the B4525 Kislingbury to Bugbrooke road a short distance west of Bugbrooke School. The present corn mill was built in 1784 after the previous mill was washed away by floods. It is two storeys high, of Northampton sand ironstone and had an internal water-wheel. In the 1930s the mill was enlarged with new buildings which used electrical power and the water-wheel was replaced by a turbine. The old watermill is now completely surrounded by the milling complex of Heygate & Sons Ltd., which started to develop in the 1940s.

57 Section of Watling Street stone tramway
SP 657562 ★

In the grass verge on the east side of the A5, 200yds north of the Bugbrooke to Litchborough road junction. This 18thC relic was reconstructed some years ago by the County Council using at least some of the original materials. The 'tramway' idea recycled Roman thinking to provide a firm surface for cart and coach wheels up a fairly lengthy gradient. The reconstructed surface consists of an approximately 10ft (3m) length of stone runners.

57 Section of Watling St tramway, Bugbrooke

BURTON LATIMER   C3

58 Former watermill
SP 888750 ❏

On a long leat from the River Ise, a little under ¼ mile north-west of the road between Burton Latimer and Isham. The site had been used for a silk mill, a woollen mill, a cotton mill and a chicory and mustard mill before Thomas Wallis erected a new flour mill in about 1880. It is of four storeys and 9 bays, with distinctive round-headed windows on the upper storey and using the latest fireproof construction which survives. In the 1930s the mill was purchased by Whitworth Bros. It is exterior clad and is now completely surrounded by the modern Weetabix production complex.

CASTLE ASHBY   C2

59 Former pump house
SP 856595 ❏ LBII

Situated on the Compton Estate at the north-east corner of the *Engine Pond*. This is located at the end of a track which heads west-north-west from the road through the village, opposite shops in the former Home Farm. The building is of banded limestone and Northampton sand ironstone, single storey facing onto the pond, but two storeys at the rear. It has a red-tiled, hipped roof and originally had an external water-wheel on the north-west side, driving pumps inside the building. During the 19thC these were replaced by large hydraulic rams which in turn were replaced by electric pumps situated in another building, now derelict, a short distance to the north-east. The pump house is now a dwelling.

60 Remains of brick kiln
SP 859600 ❏

In a spinney, less than 100yds north of the Castle Ashby to Grendon road, 100yds east of its junction with the road to Whiston. Now virtually enclosed by trees and undergrowth this rectangular updraught kiln is still intact. It was part of the Castle Ashby estate brickworks and is thought to have operated from before 1887 until WW2.

61 Former water tower
SP 862593 ❏ LBII C

In Castle Ashby grounds, on the north side of the courtyard between the stable block and the mansion. The four-storey square stone tower with a smaller staircase tower projecting from one corner was built in 1865 as part of the improved water supply for the estate. On the top is a balustrade with lettering matching that around the top of the mansion.

62 Former electricity generating house
SP 862592 ❏ C

To the west of the stable block, is a T-shaped single-storey building which used to house the electricity generating equipment for lighting the mansion. The building is of stone with a

21

red pantile roof and ball finials at the ridge of each gable. There are louvred dormers on the south side of the roof. The generating plant has been removed and the large window in the east gable end blocked with stones in converting the building to a dwelling.

CATESBY A2

63 Former Catesby tunnel and viaduct
SP 533570 – 521605 ★
Much of the infrastructure of the former Great Central Railway has now disappeared, but Catesby tunnel and viaduct still remain as examples of the significant engineering of the line, opened in 1899 and closed in 1966. The tunnel, the longest on the line at one mile 1240yds (2743m), is of blue engineering brick, with five ventilation shafts. The tunnel portals have been sealed since closure and the interior is now inaccessible. The southern portal (SP 533570) is reached by a footpath from the Charwelton to Hellidon road. The northern portal (SP 524596) is adjacent to the footpath from Upper to Lower Catesby. About one mile further north at SP 521605, the 159yd (145m) long Catesby viaduct across the Leam valley consists of 12 blue brick arches and is visible from the Jurassic Way.

CHAPEL BRAMPTON B2

64 Former agricultural implement works
SP 730663 ★
Situated at the junction of the roads to Northampton and Pitsford, the building is between two cottages of ironstone. Its ironstone gable end faces the road with, on the left, large double doors surmounted by a large fanlight and, on the right, a large cast-iron framed rectangular window. Thomas Coleman was the blacksmith here in 1841. Twenty years later his son, William, had taken over the premises as an agricultural implement maker. Later only blacksmithing was carried out here.

CHARLTON A1

65 Former watermill
SP 522354 ★
On the Charlton Brook, a tributary of the River Cherwell, less than ½ mile west of the road heading south from the village. Although in a ruinous and overgrown state, the remains of the corn mill show that an overshot water-wheel was used.

CHARWELTON A2

66 Packhorse bridge
SP 535561 ★ LBII* S
On the east side of the A361 in the village. To modern eyes, quite an elaborate bridge to cross a minor stream! Of local ironstone construction with two Gothic arches, the bridge dates from medieval times and is only wide enough for one horse to cross at a time.

67 Remains of ironstone tramway depot
SP 527568 ❑
Just inside the grounds of Manor Farm Nurseries on the Charwelton to Priors Marston road, about one mile from Charwelton. There are three corrugated iron sheds formerly used by the Park Gate Iron & Steel Company for their Charwelton Ironstone Quarries which operated in the area just south of Hellidon between 1919 and 1963. Iron ore was taken from the quarries down to the Great Central Railway at Charwelton via a standard gauge tramway which passed through the site. The

66 Packhorse bridge, Charwelton

larger two sheds contained the forge – still extant – and the engineering workshops. The third is thought to be the much-altered remains of the locoshed.

COGENHOE C2

68 Former watermill
SP 832613 ★ LBII
On the River Nene, at the end of a lane heading north from the east end of the village. The three-storey corn mill is of brick with slate roof and has a datestone of 1725. It is now devoid of machinery but was unusual for a watermill in having the three pairs of stones driven from above instead of from below. The adjoining mill house is of stone, two-storeys with a steeply pitched tiled roof.

68 Former watermill, Cogenhoe

COLLYWESTON D4

69 Former Collyweston slate workings
TF 004039 ★
Collyweston stone was mined to provide roofing slates from Roman times, with the peak of activity in the 18thC. Extracted slate 'logs' were exposed to frost in order to cleave into slates. There were workings on both sides of the A43 but most have been ploughed over. Note the name Slate Drift leading off the main road. Overgrown surface workings remain in an area now known as *The Deeps*, a nature reserve to the north of the A43 between Collyweston and Easton-on-the-Hill, through which a footpath runs (enter at TF 005036).

CORBY C4

Corby was just a village when blast furnaces first opened in 1910. It was not until 1930, that Corby began to grow, when the site was taken over by Stewarts & Lloyds and the iron & steel-making complex developed rapidly. In its heyday it was the largest industrial site in the county employing more than 6000 local people. Twice nationalised it was suddenly closed in 1979 and virtually all was swept away. Apart from the Tubeworks (now owned by Tata Steel) there is little visible evidence, the area being covered by a retail park and industrial estates.

70 Site of former steelworks
SP 900898 ★
On Phoenix Parkway to the north-east of the present town centre. A steel tube some 30ft (9m) high representing the *Corby Candle* – the exhaust pipe used to burn off waste gases – has been placed at the side of the road near the centre of the site of the steelworks.

71 Housing for steelworkers
SP 893893 ★
To the east of Rockingham Rd, north-east of the present town centre. Overlooking the site of the former steelworks, some 2,200 houses were built in the 1930s to take the large influx of workers, mainly from Glasgow, at the expanding Stewarts & Lloyds plant.

72 Statue of steelworker
SP 881885 ★
Situated outside the Corby Cube in George St. First erected in 1989, a bronze statue of a steelworker by N Grevatte is one of the few visual signs of the town's *raison d'etre*. With bronze reliefs depicting the town's history on the plinth, it was relocated in 2011 and dedicated to workers killed at the steelworks.

COSGROVE B1

73 Former brewery & maltings
SP 792425 ★ C
Situated on the south side of the road, heading south-east from the crossroads towards the canal. The brewery was in the three and two-

73 Former brewery and maltings, Cosgrove

storey buildings. These have stone lower storeys, brick above and are surmounted by slate roofs. The stone building nearest to the canal with slate roof, was the malting. The brewery was built in 1858 by Daniel Warren and in 1875 had a 10-quarter mash vat, horizontal steam engine and refrigerator. Francis Bull was the owner from 1876 to 1888 when Phipps of Northampton bought the premises. Since 1932 the premises have been used for purposes other than brewing and are now occupied by a variety of small businesses.

74 Road bridge over canal
SP 793427 ★ LBII* C
The road heading north-east from the crossroads in the village crosses the Grand Union Canal by an unusually elaborate stone bridge (No.65) built in the Gothic style and known as *Solomon's Bridge*. Such ornamentation was the result of a 'bargain' agreed between the landowner and the canal company when extra land was acquired to divert the public road to serve the village on the east side of the canal.

75 Tunnel under canal
SP 793426 ★ LBII C
At the end of the road heading south-east from the village crossroads, is a narrow tunnel

through the canal embankment which has a profile suited to the passage of canal horses between the tow-path and stables at the *Barley Mow Inn*. It was built to maintain communications between the two parts of the village when the canal bisected the main street. Road traffic was diverted to cross the canal at Solomon's Bridge.

76 Remains of canal wharf & tramway
SP 795423 ★ C
Immediately north of Cosgrove Lock are the remains of a wharf which served gravel pits, now flooded, to the east of the canal. Embedded in the concrete are narrow gauge tramway tracks.

77 Former canal junction and lock
SP 794422 ★ C
The Buckingham branch of the Grand Union Canal, opened in 1801, left the main-line of the canal in a south-westerly direction. It was disused for commercial traffic to Buckingham by 1910 but continued in use as far as Deanshanger until 1938. The whole branch was abandoned in 1961 although the first 200yds is still in water for boat moorings. The unwatered course can be followed up to the A5, north-east of Old Stratford. A little to the

south of the former canal junction is Lock No.21 with a fall of 3ft 4in (1m). It is on the site of the top lock of the temporary flight of five, which used to take the canal down to cross the River Great Ouse on the level before the present embankment and aqueduct was built in 1811 (Site 78).

78 Canal aqueduct & embankment
SP 795422 - 800418 ★ S
South of Lock No.21, the Grand Union Canal is carried on an embankment of increasing height until the River Great Ouse is crossed into Buckinghamshire by an iron aqueduct at a height of about 35ft (10m). This 'Iron Trunk' was erected in 1811 to replace the original stone culverts which collapsed in 1808. At each end of the aqueduct is a cattle-shaped tunnel through the embankment, known as a cattle creep.

78 'Iron trunk' canal aqueduct, Cosgrove

COTTERSTOCK — D4
79 Former watermill
TL 048904 ★ C
On a leat from the River Nene, at the south end of the village. The impressive three and four-storey corn mill, with ashlar walls and stone slate roof, was burnt down in 1968 although the wheel races and sluices for the two breast-shot water-wheels can still be seen. The granary building, which was at right-angles to the mill at its north-west end, has been adapted for a dwelling, its north-east end being set back from its original position alongside the road.

COTTINGHAM — C4
80 Remains of limekiln
SP 847899 ★ LBII
In a small valley on the south side of the Corby road as it enters the village from the east. This is a good example of the remains of a stone fronted limekiln built into the hillside.

81 Former Wallis clothing factory
SP 847902 ★
On Rockingham Rd at the top of the hill. The 3-storey brick-built factory, large for the size of the village, carries a datestone for1872 and was constructed as the Wallis clothing factory, later part of Wallis & Linnell. Note the carved stone faces protruding from the brickwork on the front of the building. Compare with the former Wallis factory at Brigstock (Site 51). The building has been converted to apartments but with disappointing plastic windows.

82 Parish boundary marker
SP 842901 ★ LBII
On the north side of Berry Road at its junction with Glover Court. 19thC cast-iron three-cornered post with the inscription: *Parish Boundary Cottingham / Middleton.*

CRANFORD — C3
83 Former ironstone workings /tramway
SP 931772 ★
Approached by a footpath running east from the minor road about 200yds north of the church at Cranford St John. There is evidence of a tramway which carried iron ore from the early 1920s from quarries to the north, down to a junction with the former Midland Railway's Kettering to Huntingdon line. A concrete bridge remains over the stream adjacent to the footpath and the route to North Pit is clear, as is the later diversion to Thomson's Pit, worked until 1958.

CRANSLEY — C3
84 Cransley reservoir and former pump house
SP 833782 ★
Situated west of the Cransley to Thorpe Malsor road, the dam is crossed by a public

footpath which starts from near White Hill Lodge on the road from Cransley and leads to the church at Thorpe Malsor. To the north-east of the dam is the former pump house. It consisted of three long brick buildings with ridge roofs and round-headed cast-iron window frames together with a square brick chimney with stone top. This has been converted to a private dwelling and the walls are now rendered white. On the south side of the entrance to the site from the Cransley to Thorpe Malsor road is the former water-works superintendent/engineer's house. This is also now a private residence.

CRICK A3

85 Milestone
SP 586724 ★
In the grass verge on the south side of Main Rd at the western edge of the village. A lime-stone milestone approximately 3ft x 1ft 6in x 6in (1m x 0.5m x 15cm) in a semi-dressed state. A replacement cast-iron distance marker was affixed in 2003.

86 Former wharf house, Crick

86 Canal wharf
SP 596725 ★ C
Crick Wharf is adjacent to the south side of the A428 which crosses the Leicester line of the Grand Union Canal on bridge No.12. On the opposite side of the wharf area from the canal is a rare example of a little-altered wharf house (LBII). Two-storey brick warehouses are alongside the road but have been altered for other uses. For a period during the 20thC, concrete piles were cast in the warehouses

and moved out into the yard on wagons running on a rail system with turntables. The wharf area is still in use for pleasure craft today,

87 Crick canal tunnel north entrance
SP 595721 ★ LBII C
Approached by the tow-path which heads south from the bridge taking the A428 over the Leicester line of the Grand Union Canal, is the north entrance to the Crick Tunnel, opened in 1814. It is 1528yds (1397m) long and is brick-lined but without tow-path or ventilation shafts. However, there are 10 distinct mounds of excavated material from the construction of the tunnel, in a straight line between the two tunnel mouths. One mound is immediately to the north of the Crick to Watford road (SP 592710).

88 Crick canal tunnel south entrance
SP 592707 ★ LBII C
The south entrance to Crick tunnel (see Site 87) is reached by a track heading south-west from the Crick to Watford road, just south of Limes Farm. The accommodation bridge, 20m south of the tunnel entrance, is also LBII.

CROUGHTON A1

89 Former watermill
SP 540332 ★
On the Croughton Brook, a tributary of the River Cherwell, located on the west side of the lane running south from the B4031 at the west end of the village. This small two-storey, stone-built corn mill with slate roof was at one time driven by steam as well as water.

CULWORTH A1

90 Blacksmith's forge
SP 543470 ★ C LBII
Situated on the south side of High Street, a little west of the street called Banbury Lane is Culworth forge. This is a single-storey stone building with a brick lean-to extension along the side onto the road, with a continuous window for most of its length. It now operates as part of Culworth Engineering Ltd. which has other premises close to the forge.

DAVENTRY · A2

The town's importance in the 18thC was due to its position on the Great Chester Road (later the Holyhead Road); it diminished when the development of the railways reduced long-distance road traffic. The leather craft activities associated with the latter provided a basis for the 19thC footwear industry in the town. This ended in the last decades of the 20thC as did transmissions from the nationally significant high-power radio station 5XX on Borough Hill which started in 1925. Surprisingly little physical evidence remains of past industrial activities in the town; the thriving present-day industries are all in modern buildings.

91 Milestone and cast-iron mileage plate
SP 576617 ★
Situated at the north-west corner of the junction of London Rd and The Slade. One of the milestones erected in the 1820s along the route of Thomas Telford's London to Holyhead road. The stone is dressed to the front and sides but rough-hewn to the rear. The original cast-iron plate, by Tarver's Daventry Foundry, measures approximately 2ft x 1ft 6in (0.6m x 0.4m). It shows distances to: *London 71 miles, Daventry ½ mile* and *Towcester 11½ miles.*

92 Former railway branch line
SP 566643 – 591614 ★
A branch line was opened by the LNWR from their main line at Weedon, reaching Daventry in 1888 and later being extended to serve Leamington. Several features remain around Daventry, where part of the trackbed is utilised as a footpath. Bridges remain where the former trackbed passes beneath Ashby Rd (SP 569641) and beneath a minor road near Borough Hill Farm (SP 592614). There are also bridges over Welton Rd (SP 574637 although here the original span has been replaced) and over a track adjacent to Northern Way (SP 575635). In addition there is a concrete gradient post alongside the footpath at SP 576632 and what is probably the remains of the base of a goods yard crane on the site of Daventry station on the west side of South

92 Concrete gradient post, Daventry

Way at SP 577626. The line was closed to passengers in 1958 and to freight traffic in December 1963.

93 Canal reservoir
SP 569648 ★
The dam for Drayton (or Daventry Old) reservoir is along the west side of the A361 to Kilsby, just north of the roundabout on the Daventry north ring road. When full, the water covers 27 acres and is fed by streams from the west and north. It was built to hold water for about 1,300 locks to supply the summit level of the Grand Junction (later Grand Union) Canal when it opened in 1796.

94 Canal reservoir
SP 576642 ★
A low earth dam is at the north end of Daventry reservoir and can be reached from the car park, entered from the A425 just south of the roundabout at its junction with the Welton road. It was built on the line of the proposed Daventry Branch Canal, which was never constructed. It held water for more than 6,000 locks to supplement the original reservoir at Daventry and opened in 1804, covering 100 acres. Now part of Daventry Country Park.

96 Former Roberts foundry, Deanshanger

Roberts, the company made portable horse engines, agricultural implements and wind-operated pumps until 1929. Around the village and further afield are cast-iron items such as wall ties carrying the Roberts name. Subsequently the site was used for the production of oxides and other pigments for paints, the most recent owner Elementis, closed in 1999. The rest of the site has been cleared for housing development and the surviving buildings are awaiting refurbishment, a request to demolish them having been recently refused.

95 Braunston canal tunnel entrance
SP 575651 ★ C

The east entrance to Braunston Tunnel is reached by following the tow-path through a wooded cutting from the Daventry to Watford road where it crosses the Grand Union Canal about ½ mile south of Welton. A mistake during the construction of the tunnel gives it a slight 'S' bend but from a point on the tow-path some distance east of this entrance in certain conditions it is possible to see to the other end (see also Site 48).

DEANSHANGER   B1
96 Remains of Roberts agricultural implement works
SP 764397 ★ C

On the north side of High St less than 300yds north of the junction with Stratford Rd are the surviving buildings of the former Roberts' engineering business. Except for the stone north gable end, the larger building is of red brick, two-storeys high with five bays and elaborate cast-iron window frames. Adjacent to the south side is a single-storey red brick building, of almost the same height as the first. A foundry was established here in 1847 by John Roberts. The first of the above buildings was built about 1860. Later, trading as E & H

DENFORD   D3
97 Remains of brick kiln
SP 998769 ★

A narrow lane leads east off the Denford to Thrapston road about ¼ mile north of Denford. The remains of the kiln, now incorporated into stabling for horses, are in a field to the south-east of the road bridge over the former Midland Railway's Kettering to Huntingdon line. The kiln is approximately 15ft (4.5m) square and roofless. It was known to be working between 1877 and 1885. There is evidence of quarrying/spoil in the vicinity.

DESBOROUGH   C3
98 Former shoe factory
SP 802835 ★ C

Situated behind the more modern brick and rendered 2-storey plus basement building in Gladstone St, off the east side of Harborough Rd. The 2-storey plus basement, 18-bay brick-built factory with cast-iron windows, possibly the longest of its type in the county, is thought to date from the 1860s or 1870s and was originally used as a shoe factory. Subsequently used by RS Lawrence, leather and component suppliers, but is now empty and under threat of demolition.

28

99 Cheaney shoe factory
SP 807835 ★ LBII

On the south side of Rushton Rd just east of its junction with Pipewell Rd. Joseph Cheaney & Sons first built a shoe factory on the site in 1896 and the original eight-bay 2-storey range with cast-iron window frames backing onto Regent St is of that date. The nine-bay 2-storey brick-built range fronting onto Rushton Road is stylistically of the 1930s, with later additions. In between is a single-storey range with north-lit roof. Cheaney still manufactures footwear on the site.

100 Former Co-op corset factory
SP 801828 ★

On Rothwell Rd at its junction with Federation Avenue, south of the town centre. This extensive brick-built factory dating from 1905 was built for the Co-operative Wholesale Society as a corset and lingerie factory. It is on a total of four floors arranged to accommodate the slope of the ground up Federation Avenue. The name is picked out in white brick on the parapet fronting the factory; the letters CWS are in white brick on each face of the chimney. Now occupied by Eveden Ltd.

101 Former bus garage
SP 801834 ★

On the western side of Harborough Road in the centre of the town. An extensive (for a town this size) functional garage with a brown brick façade, built by Thomas Higgs of Northampton in 1925 for United Counties Omnibus Co. at a cost of £9,036.13s.4d. It was closed in 1978 and its future is currently uncertain.

102 Former Desborough & Rothwell station
SP 804836 ★ C

Situated on Gladstone St, ¼ mile east of the bridge carrying Harborough Rd over the railway at Desborough. The station opened in 1857 on the Midland Railway's Leicester to Hitchin extension. The station buildings are of local ironstone (compare with the former Glendon & Rushton station - Site 364), with Norman-style decorated windows framed in polychrome brick. The gables have decorated bargeboards but the finials are missing. The station closed to passengers in 1968 and is converted to a dwelling.

103 Milestone
SP 802833 ★ LBII

In High St, opposite its junction with Station Rd. Known as Desborough Town Cross, this obelisk is some 15ft (4.5m) high, of square cross-section constructed of stone blocks, on a plinth and with a stone ball on top. Tradition says that it was once part of the entrance gates to Harrington Hall, demolished in 1745. Distances in miles to *Kettering, 'Harbro'* and *London* can be made out on three faces.

99 Cheaney shoe factory, Desborough

104 Heritage Centre
SP 804835 ○ C

On the north side of Station Rd, just west of its junction with Gladstone St. Situated in a single-storey building with a false two-storey façade that was previously the Co-operative Outfitters and Hardware Store and part of which started life as Bosworth's shoe factory. Desborough Heritage Centre has an extensive photographic archive of the town's industrial past as well as limited displays of artefacts. Open Mon-Sat.
(www.desboroughheritagecentre.co.uk)

DINGLEY B4

105 Water pumps
SP 771874 ★ LBII

Situated north of the A427 and on the east side of Church Lane, which leads north to Dingley Park. An approximately 5ft 6in (1.7m) tall obelisk-like cast-iron pump with spout directed towards the lane stands beside a tubular cast-iron pump with a fluted top with spout facing to the side of the lane.

DODFORD A2

106 Former watermill
SP 610594 ☐ LBII

Originally fed from a pond served by a long leat from the River Nene, this corn mill is at the end of a private track heading west from the Dodford to Everdon road. A brick three-storey building with a slate roof, it has a date-stone of 1836 in the gable end. A steam engine was installed here in 1865. The mill was last used in 1947 and allowed to deteriorate until acquired by new owners who have converted it to a dwelling whilst retaining much of the original layout of the mill as well as most of the machinery.

DUDDINGTON D4

107 Former watermill
SK 986009 ★ LBII

On the River Welland, south-east of the road passing the church to join the A47 west of the village. Once the location for an experiment in textiles, this fine stone building – a former corn mill – has a stone-slated mansard roof. An arch carries a two-storey projection over the wheel race. Dates of 1614 and 1729 are recorded on a stone in one wall. The mill was disused by 1922 and is now used as offices.

108 Cast-iron boundary marker
SK 985009 ★

On the medieval bridge (LBII S) over the River Welland which carries the road passing the church to join the A47 west of the village. A 19thC cast-iron boundary marker at the centre of the bridge denotes the boundary between the parishes of Duddington and Tixover (Rutland).

EARLS BARTON C2

109 Former WJ Brookes shoe factory
SP 854643 ★

In King Street off Wilby Rd, ½ mile north-east of The Square. WJ Brookes built this 14-bay, three-storey red brick shoe factory in 1889 with a later 2-storey extension. The factory operated under the same name until mid-2000, shortly after being in the news for identifying a niche market in manufacturing 'kinky boots'. This was later the subject of a 2005 feature film (see also Site 268). A wall-mounted crane still exists adjacent to the 1st floor doors in the 2-storey extension. Since closure, the buildings have been converted to apartments although there are now ugly plastic windows.

107 Former watermill, Duddington

110 Former Ward & Sheffield shoe factory
SP 852637 ★

In Harcourt Square off Station Rd, immediately south of The Square. The three-storey brick-built shoe factory constructed c1900 was the home of Ward & Sheffield until the 1960s. It was subsequently used by W Botterill (Gola) for additional manufacturing capacity for three years from 1967. Now converted to apartments, the wall-mounted crane remains adjacent to the former 1st floor doors.

111 Former shoe outworkers' workshops
SP 848636 ★
In Sunnyside, off Park St, ¼ mile west of The Square. A terrace of cottages dates from 1886, with single-storey extensions forming workshops, adjacent to the road. They were used by shoe outworkers for cutting and stitching operations. Earlier workshops are behind houses in Park St (SP 849637 ❏).

112 Former goods shed
SP 859617 ★
On the Earls Barton to Grendon road approximately ¼ mile south of the River Nene crossing. At the site of the former *Castle Ashby and Earls Barton* station on the LNWR's Northampton to Peterborough line opened in 1845 and closed in 1966. The brick-built goods shed, still with wooden canopy, has been converted into a restaurant retaining much of the original structure. Old railway carriages are also integrated into the building.

113 Earls Barton Museum of Village Life
SP 853637 ○
In Jeyes chemist shop on the north-east side of The Square. Includes artefacts relating to shoemaking and other local industry.

EAST CARLTON C4
114 Industrial Heritage Centre
SP 833894 ○ LBII
In the Country Park, the entrance of which is opposite the church in East Carlton village, ¼ mile north of the A427. The Industrial Heritage Centre is in the former coach house and concentrates on the history of Corby steelworks. There are also a variety of outdoor exhibits, including a steel-casting ladle, various ingots and moulds, a bucket from a W1400 walking dragline and a former industrial steam loco. (tel: 01536 770977)

EAST HADDON B2
115 Former bakery
SP 670682 ★
On the north side of the road from Holdenby and a short distance west of the *Red Lion*

Hotel. The two-storey, red-brick building with round cast-iron tie-plates each side of the top of the ground floor window and an unfenestrated projection to the east was Craddock's bakery. Baking ceased in the early 1970s but the bakehouse interior remains as it was at that time.

116 Former water tower
SP 667681 ★
Located behind the post office, south of the road from Holdenby that passes the church. A small, stone, circular tower surmounted by a conical tiled roof. Large hydraulic rams pumped water to the tank in the tower from the brook which passes under the road going north from the village towards Ravensthorpe. The rams were removed many years ago.

116 Former water tower, East Haddon

EASTON NESTON B1
117 Former railway bridge
SP 713504 ★
Reached via a bridleway running south of the Tiffield to Shutlanger road, ¼ mile east of its junction with the A43. This is a good example of an accommodation bridge, beneath the former trackbed of the Towcester to Ravenstone Wood Junction section of the Stratford and Midland Junction Railway. Opened in 1891, the bridge has a brick arch with stone

spandrels, blue-brick capped revetments and still retains the railings at track level. It is in remarkably good condition considering the line closed as a through route in 1958 when severed by the construction of the M1 motorway.

EASTON-ON-THE-HILL D4

118 Remains of ironstone tramway incline
TF 004056 ❑

Near the byway from Easton-on-the-Hill to Tinwell, approximately 200yds west of the railway level crossing. The incline can be seen which carried iron ore in narrow-gauge wagons from quarries at the top of the hill to the Midland Railway's Syston to Peterborough line at the bottom. At the base of the incline are the remains of the tippler, including 2 rusting steel hods used to transfer ore from narrow gauge wagons to standard gauge wagons, and the remains of the weighbridge. Further up the hill (TF 005048) are the remains of the brake wheel at the top of the incline and the locoshed. The site is owned by Burghley Estates.

119 Former windmill
TF 009037 ★

South of the A43 at the south-west end of the village. Although very overgrown with foliage, the shell of this tower corn mill is at its original height of three-storeys. Stone-built with cement rendering and then tarred, much of the latter is flaking off. When at work it had one pair of sprung-shuttered sails and the other pair had cloth-covered common sails. By 1884 it was shown as *Old Windmill* on the OS map, and now is in a ruinous condition.

120 Former Stamford racecourse
TF 021038 to 035041 ★

South of the minor road running east from Easton-on-the-Hill to the A1. A one mile long strip of land 40-75yds (35-70m) wide, bounded for the most part by modern hedges and representing the second (1820s) racecourse on the site. The track stretches just into Cambridgeshire where the 1766 grandstand was situated at the winning post. This building (LBII*) remains and is now a dwelling. The straight track replaced an earlier oval course of which no remains are extant save for hedges bounding the complete site as a rectangle. A public footpath passes the west end of the site whilst the east end is fairly near the road.

120 Former grandstand for Stamford Racecourse, Easton-on-the-Hill

FINEDON C3

121 Former windmill
SP 907724 ★ LBII

On the south-west side of the minor road to Burton Latimer is a 4-storey tower mill of Northampton sand ironstone built in 1818 for milling corn. In about 1850 the mill was converted to a residence, *Exmill Cottage*, the architect EF Law giving it the present Gothic style to meet William Mackworth-Dolben's wishes. The large extension on the north side was built in the 1960s.

122 Remains of ironstone workings
SP 911722 ★

Access off the minor road from Finedon to Burton Latimer, 200yds north-west of Finedon church. Now a Pocket Park, these were formerly the quarries for Richard Thomas & Co. which were worked between 1936 and 1960. Bridge parapets remain where the standard gauge tramway tunnelled beneath the road. To the west, the line of the tramway can be easily seen. This transported iron ore from quarries east of the road down to the Midland Main

Line. The remains of calcine banks at the foot of the incline close to the River Ise (SP 902712) are now a nature reserve. To the east, the Pocket Park follows ironstone gullets for ½ mile with remains of wooden and concrete sleepers. At the south-east end of the quarry (SP 915722) is the entrance to the tunnel (now bricked up) which carried a narrow-gauge electric underground tramway for transporting ore under Finedon Hill to the processing plant at Irthlingborough, some 2 miles away. The tunnel was in use from 1939 until about 1945.

123 Former Arthur Nutt shoe factory, Finedon

123 Former Arthur Nutt shoe factory
SP 916718 ★
On the north side of Wellingborough Rd, about ¼ mile west of its junction with the A6. Attractive three-storey shoe factory dates from 1903, with later single-storey extensions demolished and replaced by new 3-storey apartment blocks. Original building is of red brick with white and blue brick banding and white brick window arches and is now converted to apartments, the new black window frames looking better than those on similar conversions elsewhere. Occupied by Arthur Nutt up until the 1970s, then by the Tower Boot Co. who were later incorporated into the R Griggs Group (see Site 444). Footwear production ceased in mid-2000.

124 Former wool-stapling business
SP 921723 ★
On the east side of the A6 Burton Rd, approximately 150yds north of its junction with the A510. A four-bay single-storey north-lit range with limestone walls and an attractive road frontage with shaped gables. Behind is a roughly contemporary 3-storey brick range with hipped roof. Built sometime after 1893 by Francis Sharp for his wool-stapling business and subsequently used at different times for shoe manufacturing and leather finishing. Most recently was the office and closing room of the Rockleigh Shoe Co. until c2000. Now used by Carmac Ltd.

125 Former water tower
SP 925718 ★ LBII
On the north-east side of Irthlingborough Rd, near the southern edge of Finedon. The five-storey, octagonal, polychrome-brick water tower was built in 1904. Following extensive internal work, it is now a dwelling.

126 Former clothing factory
SP 925718 ★
On the north-east side of Irthlingborough Rd, immediately south of the former water tower (Site 125). Six single-storey north-lit ranges built as a satellite factory c1910 for Wellingborough-based Ideal Clothiers. Constructed of brick, the gables have oculi with bull-nosed brick surrounds. The façade to the road is pebble-dashed. Now used by a caravan sales company. A similar design of factory built for the same company is located in Station Rd Burton Latimer.

FLORE   B2
127 Former wheelwright and wagon builder's workshops
SP 643603 ★
On the north side of the A45 opposite Spring Lane are the premises of the former wagon and wheelwright business of the Phillips family. The last wagon was made in 1921 although horse-box trailers and similar were produced here until the 1980s. The main building is of brick with a corrugated metal roof.

128 Former whip factory
SP 646603 ★ LBII

On the east side of Sutton St in the curtilage of No. 7 *The White Cottage*, are buildings associated with the whip making business of Henry Sharp. One is thought to have been built soon after 1833 when the making of whips in Flore expanded. Next to it is a single-storey brick building dating from the third quarter of the 19thC, also part of the whip factory which by 1871 employed 10 people. The last whips were made here a few years after WWI. Both buildings were re-roofed c1966 following a fire.

131 Canal turnover bridge, Gayton

129 Former watermill
SP 644596 ★

On the River Nene, on the west of the junction of the two roads heading south from the village. The two-storey brick building was originally the corn mill, and the three-storey building adjoining it on the north side, was the mill house.

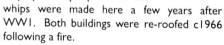

FOTHERINGHAY   D4

130 Road bridge over River Nene
TL 060930 ★ C S

The present bridge, south-east of the church dates from 1722 and was designed by George Portwood, a Stamford architect. It has 4 semi-circular arches, all at different heights. Stone from the King's Cliffe quarries was used in its construction.

GAYTON   B2

131 Canal 'turnover' bridge
SP 717553 ★ LBII

Combined with the bridge carrying the Rothersthorpe to Gayton road over the Grand Union Canal is a second bridge known as Turnover Bridge No.47. This was specially constructed to take the tow-path over the canal. The ramps were suitable for horses to cross and their position on the same side of the bridge enabled boats to pass under the bridge without unhitching the tow-rope.

132 Former ironstone tramway tunnel
SP 712538 ★

On the Gayton to Blisworth road, 150yds west of its junction with the Rothersthorpe to Tiffield road. Richard Thomas and Baldwin operated a standard gauge tramway from the former Stratford & Midland Junction Railway to its Blisworth Quarries from c1943 to 1967. Where it passed beneath the road, a concrete square cross-section tunnel remains, with parapets at road level almost hidden by vegetation.

GEDDINGTON   C3

133 Conduit house
SP 894830 ★ C

Stands in juxtaposition with the Eleanor Cross (LBI) in the centre of the village. It was built in 1769 to supply the village with water and the rectangular stone chamber is still intact.

134 Road bridge over River Ise and ford
SP 894829 ★ LBII* S

In the village centre, south of the Eleanor Cross. The present bridge, though much repaired, dates largely from the 13thC. It boasts two pointed arches, one round arch (from alterations in 1784) and large cutwaters. The ford immediately adjacent is still maintained and provides an alternative to the bridge for the more adventurous traveller!

GREAT DODDINGTON C2

135 Former Hardwater watermill
SP 876636 ★ LBII
On the River Nene, west of the Wollaston to Great Doddington road. In the 14thC it was known as *Hepdewath* but by the early 18thC, maps show it as *Hardwater Mill*. The former two-storey stone built corn mill is at the south-west end of the range of buildings. It ceased work c1930.

GREAT OAKLEY C3

136 Former Geddington station
SP 875852 ★
Adjacent to the Great Oakley to Little Oakley road about ½ mile east of the turn for Newton and Geddington. On the Midland Railway's Kettering to Manton line, *Geddington* station is two miles as the crow flies from the village whose name it bears. Opened in 1879, the station building is of brick, with a steeply pitched roof. The bargeboards on the gables are plain (compare with the earlier station at Rushton - Site 364) but there are finials on the ridge. Closed in 1948, the building is a dwelling but can be clearly seen from the road.

137 Railway viaduct
SP 881857 ★
Visible from the Great Oakley to Little Oakley road, about one mile west of Little Oakley. This ten-arch brick viaduct was built in the late 1870s to carry the Midland Railway's Kettering to Manton line over Harper's Brook. Following the reopening of Corby station in 2009, the line once again carries both passenger and freight traffic.

GRETTON C4

138 Former Gretton station
SP 895941 ★
Adjacent to the viaduct taking the railway over the Rockingham to Gretton road near to its junction with the road to Lyddington. Opened in 1879 on the Midland Railway's Kettering to Manton line, the station building is single-storey. Unusually, it is of stone construction to a classical design more akin to the London & Birmingham Railway. Steps from the road to the non-existent platforms ascend either side of the viaduct. A foot tunnel halfway up connects the two. The station was closed in 1966 and is now a dwelling.

HARLESTONE B2

139 Remains of stone quarries
SP 705640 ★
The main quarries are adjacent to the south side of the road leading from the A428 to Upper Harlestone but earlier, probably medieval, quarries lie to the north (SP 705644). Harlestone quarries were the source of sandstone for many of Northampton's buildings.

140 Horse trough
SP 704646 ★ C
On the west side of the A428, a little south of the turn to Church Brampton. A monumental trough for use by horses ascending the steep slope north of Lower Harlestone. It was erected in 1904 by the husband of Charlotte Countess Spencer who died in 1903. She '....*for gods dumb creatures cared*....' according to the long inscription above the trough.

135 Former Hardwater watermill, Great Doddington

144 Harringworth viaduct

141 Remains of brick kiln
SP 695642 ▢

In a spinney immediately to the north of Upper Harlestone are the remains of a rectangular brick kiln, approximately 25ft by 15ft (8m by 5m), much overgrown. The walls are reinforced by lengths of rail, driven into the ground. Known operating dates are 1883-1901, although it was never shown in directories. Access only with permission of Spencer Estates.

142 Former Dovecote laundry
SP 692640 ★

West of the road to Brington, beyond a dovecote after which the laundry was named when it was operating. A single-storey building of red brick with slate roof. It had a Marshall single-cylinder, horizontal steam engine driving laundry machinery via belts from an overhead shaft. All this was removed when the building was adapted for other use.

HARRINGTON · B3
143 Water pump
SP 775802 ★ C

Situated in the wide grass verge on the south-east side of the road to Lamport, a short distance south-west from the *Tollemache Arms* is a cast-iron hand pump.

HARRINGWORTH · C4
144 Harringworth (Welland) Viaduct
SP 913969 to SP 914981 ★ LBII

Dominating the landscape to the west and north of Harringworth village. The viaduct was built in the late 1870s by the Midland Railway to connect Kettering to Manton across the valley of the River Welland and thus provide an alternative route from St Pancras to Nottingham through Oakham and Melton Mowbray. Following a long period as a freight-only route – except when Sunday diversion trains used it, the line is again used by scheduled through passenger trains now that Corby station has reopened. At 1275yds (1166m) long, it is the longest masonry viaduct across a valley in Britain. It has 82 arches, each 40ft (12m) wide and at its highest is 60ft (18m) from parapet to ground. It is built of blue brick reputedly manufactured on site, although much of the repair work is red brick. One third of its length is in the adjacent County of Rutland. There are good views of the viaduct at close quarters from the various roads and footpaths which criss-cross beneath the arches. A good distant view can be obtained by approaching Harringworth on the road from Gretton.

145 Commemorative stone
SP 911961 ★

Set back some 10 feet (3m) from the north side of the Harringworth to Gretton road, one mile from Harringworth church, at the south-west end of the section of road that runs parallel to the railway. Memorial stone to Fanny Maria Blaydes who was killed when her carriage overturned on the bend in 1884 after the horse was frightened by a train on the adjacent Midland Railway's Kettering to Manton line. The stone carries her initials and the date of her death.

HELLIDON   A2

146 Former windmill
SP 519577 ★ LBII
At the end of a track running east from the road which heads south from the village to the Priors Marston - Charwelton road. Built in 1842 of red brick and rendered, this three-storey tower mill had four common cloth sails and a fantail, and worked four pairs of stones to mill corn. The mill ceased work c1905 but still contained much of its wooden machinery until 1975 when it was converted to a dwelling and the aluminium dome was fitted at that time.

HELMDON   A1

147 Stained glass window
commemorating stone mason
SP 590432 ○ LBII*
In St Mary Magdalene Church Helmdon, at the east end of the north wall. Dated as1313, the stained-glass window commemorates William Campiun, a stonemason and shows him wielding his hammer. Remounted in recent years, the original lead is retained in a wall frame close-by.

148 Former Helmdon (GC) station and goods shed
SP 586431 ★
At the southern end of Helmdon village on the road toward Brackley, where the road takes a sharp turn over the former Great Central Railway trackbed. Opened in 1899, Helmdon station was of a typical GC pattern, the island platform being accessed from the road bridge. The platform is just about visible from the north side of the road bridge although covered in trees. Closer to the village, the stationmaster's house is still a dwelling and adjacent are the remains of the brick-built goods shed and weighbridge. Helmdon station closed in 1963.

149 Former railway viaduct
SP 583437 ★
Immediately to the west of Helmdon village and visible from roads to the north. Between 1899 and 1966, this nine-arch blue-brick viaduct carried the Great Central Railway over a stream and the trackbed of the former Stratford and Midland Junction Railway.

150 Former Helmdon (SMJ) goods shed
SP 588438 ★
In Helmdon village 200yds south of the junction of the roads to Sulgrave and Wappenham and east of the bridge which carried the road over the former trackbed of the Stratford and Midland Junction Railway. The brick goods shed, which until recently retained its projecting wooden canopy, is adjacent to the site of Helmdon station (opened 1871, closed 1951). It is now part of a coach depot.

150 Former SMJ goods shed, Helmdon

151 Former Astwell watermill
SP 608445 ★
On south side of the Helmdon to Wappenham road, just west of the turn to Astwell Castle. The two-storey brick building was a corn mill. The mill pond on the south side fed an iron overshot water-wheel (removed by 1970) driving three pairs of stones. From 1885 until 1940 steam power was used as well as the water-wheel. Now converted to a dwelling.

HIGHAM FERRERS   C2

152 Remains of brickworks
SP 952686 ★
In undergrowth adjacent to a footpath, approx. 100yds south of the bridge at the west end of Wharf Road Higham Ferrers. There are the remains of a brick-built circular wash pit, about 10ft (3m) diameter, with adjacent supporting walls. It was part of Wharf Lane

Brickworks which operated between 1849 and 1927, bricks being transported from the adjacent wharf on the River Nene.

153 Former headquarters of John White Footwear Ltd.
SP 962686 ★ C
On the east side of Midland Rd, immediately to the east of the town centre. The two-storey brick-built office block with central stone façade was completed in 1936 as the headquarters for John White Footwear Ltd. It is currently awaiting redevelopment. Adjacent on its south side is a more impressive single-storey office block, the remains of the shoe factory built by Charles Parker in 1906, used as offices for John White from 1936 until the 1970s. It has a projecting semicircular stone porch, with columns and stone facings to the windows on each side. Immediately opposite is John White Court, consisting of post-war bungalows built for retired shoe-workers.

HOLDENBY   B2
154 Former watermill
SP 704689 ★
Situated alongside the Spratton Brook, a tributary of the River Nene North Water, and on the north-west side of the Holdenby to Spratton road. Formerly a corn mill, this is a fine two-storey building in brown stone, almost uniform across mill and mill house. The window and door lintels are of a lighter stone, as is the string course which incorporates the sills of the upper floor windows. A single-storey building adjoining the south-west end formerly housed the water-wheel. All machinery has been removed.

IRCHESTER   C2
155 Former steam mill
SP 901665 ★
At Little Irchester, on the south-east side of the River Nene just east of the A509 Wellingborough to Olney road. *Victoria Mills*, a red-brick, four-storey building was built in 1886 for John Bathams Whitworth. Despite its situation by the river, the mill never used water power but started production using a steam

engine to drive roller milling plant. Steam power was replaced by electricity in 1958-59 and the tall chimney demolished. The location of the mill was ideal for the transport of the day being situated between important roads, the LNWR's Northampton to Peterborough line and the river, the latter being used to deliver grain from London docks to the mills until 1969. The building is still part of Whitworth Bros. premises.

155 Former steam mill, Little Irchester

156 Twin railway viaducts
SP 921673 ★
Reached via a footpath along the north bank of the River Nene from either The Embankment (1½ miles) or from Irthlingborough Rd, Wellingborough (1 mile). Twin viaducts take the Midland Main Line across the River Nene between Irchester and Wellingborough. The west viaduct dates from 1857 when the Midland Railway's Leicester to Hitchin extension opened. The east viaduct was built to facilitate four-track working which commenced in 1886. Both viaducts are of brick but the later one has a steel girder section across the river.

157 Remains of ironstone workings and industrial railway museum
SP 912658 ○
In Irchester Country Park off the B570 Gipsy Lane Irchester, ½ mile east of its junction with the A509. The country park comprises the remains of Irchester Ironstone Company's

Wembley Pit worked until WW2, and covers approximately 200 acres. A variety of ironstone quarry features remain, including tramway routes, calcine clamps and the impressive final face of the gullet. The park also houses the Irchester Narrow Gauge Railway Museum (www.ingrt.freeuk.com) featuring a length of metre-gauge demonstration railway track and a selection of industrial locos, wagons and other artefacts, as well as displays about ironstone quarrying.

158 Former Irchester Boot & Shoe Co. factory
SP 926656 ★
On the north side of East St, off Farndish Road Irchester. The three-storey shoe factory was built in 1892 and used by Irchester Boot & Shoe Co. In WW1 it was used as a canning factory for Parsons and afterwards as a shoe factory by Craddock Bros, later Craddock & Martin Ltd. It is now converted to apartments but retains the crane adjacent to the former loading doors.

159 Former Irchester station house and goods shed
SP 932660 ★
On the eastern side of the Midland Main Line just north of the B569 Irchester to Rushden road. Irchester station was opened in 1857,

closing in 1960. The brick-built station house remains, together with the conventional brick-built goods shed, which has a covered loading bay integral with the roof structure.

160 Ditchford bridge
SP 930683 ★ LBII S
Carries the road linking the A45 with the B571 Wellingborough to Irthlingborough road over the River Nene. Medieval road bridge of ironstone and limestone with 6 semicircular arches and cutwaters. Carries datestone of 1330/1927 and has been much restored. Approached from each side by a causeway of 3 semi-circular arches.

IRTHLINGBOROUGH C3

161 Houses associated with former coachbuilding works
SP 941712 ★
On the east side of Finedon Rd, 1½ miles north-west of the town cross. Four houses, in two pairs remain, either side of the former main entrance to the coachbuilding works of the Wellingborough Motor Omnibus Co. (pro-genitor of United Counties Omnibus Co.) as its first purpose-built base and brought into use in 1914. The houses are of the same date, one pair sporting a datestone, with *WMOCo.* lettering. Used for coachbuilding until c1950, the works buildings were demolished in 2011.

162 Former Excelsior Boot & Shoe Works
SP 943706 ★
On the north side of Victoria St, ¼ mile west of the town cross. This large three-storey brick-built factory was constructed in 1893 for JP Horn & O Partridge. It was later used by F Norton and Sons until 1958 and is now converted to apartments.

163 Former Hobbs & Co. Victoria Works leather factory
SP 942705 ★
On the north side of Victoria Rd at its junction with Queen St. Built in 1900, this leather factory originally had a mixture of

161 Datestone on former offices of coach-building works, Finedon Rd, Irthlingborough

single, two and three-storey buildings. The single-storey range fronting Victoria Rd has stone-lined, semi-circular windows. The two-storey brick office block has an elaborate stone frontage. Used in recent years both as a leather and a shoe factory.

164 Former roller skating rink
SP 952709 ★
On the north side of Station Rd just west of its junction with the A6. This plain, low, brick building was erected in the late 1930s by Stan Smith, a local garage proprietor, to cash in on the latest roller-skating craze. The building had its own oil-engine generated electricity supply and a splendid maple floor, still in-situ. Used for a variety of purposes since the onset of WW2 and currently a carpet showroom.

165 Road viaduct over River Nene
SP 956705 ★
Carries the A6 over the River Nene between Irthlingborough and Higham Ferrers. This impressive 1936 reinforced concrete structure survives in almost unaltered form. It was designed by Kettering architects, Gotch, Saunders and Surridge and opened by government minister Hore-Belisha. When built, it spanned the River Nene, two lesser water courses and the LNWR's Northampton to Peterborough line.

166 Road bridge over River Nene
SP 957706 ★ LBI S
Immediately to the east of the A6 road viaduct (Site 165). The medieval bridge of ten arches dating from the 14thC, has variously pointed and round arches. Refuges and cutwaters abound. A 1920s scheme to widen the bridge and its approaches was abandoned half-way through when it was found that the entire bridge was on the move seawards!

165 Road viaduct over River Nene, Irthlingborough

ISHAM   C3

167 Remains of watermill
SP 888742 ★
Situated at the end of Mill Road, Isham on the River Ise. By the 16thC a fulling mill had been added to the original corn mill. In the early 18thC it was entirely used for fulling but from c1750 until c1820, paper was made in the mill. For a short time it operated as a silk mill but in 1834 when in use as a carpet mill it was destroyed by fire. After rebuilding, the water-wheel was augmented by a steam engine for worsted spinning. From about 1855 until shortly after 1930 the mill was used for flour milling and then for gristing. The mill was of stone with a ridged pantiled roof. Although demolished some years ago the stone wall of the downstream side of the mill survives up to a height of about 10 feet, the openings for doors and windows being bricked up. Also surviving is the two-storey brick warehouse on the opposite side of the footpath. There are few windows except on the side facing the water but in the other side and in the gable end facing the mill are iron sliding doors. The slate roof has almost gone.

168 Footbridge over railway
SP 889743 ★
The footpath between Isham and Burton Latimer is carried over the Midland Main Line

by a riveted lattice-work footbridge. It is reached by stone steps, with a landing half-way up, supported by substantial red and blue brick structures. On the east side of the railway the steps rise from north of the bridge, whilst on the west they rise from the south.

169 Former water tower
SP 870734 ★
On the north side of the Isham to Orlingbury road, about 1mile from Isham. A brick structure of 3 bays by 2 bays, each bay has the first storey open and surmounted by a brick arch. To lift water into the tank, which supplied the village of Isham, there was a windpump on top, of which only the pylon survives.

ISLIP   D3
170 Vent shaft for former underground iron ore workings
SP 971792 ★
Close to the footpath which heads due west from Islip village and 200yds east of the byway from Woodford to Lowick. A brick ventilation chimney approx. 16ft (5m) high and 8ft (2.5m) in diameter used to vent Islip Iron Co.'s Church Mine some 100ft (30m) below ground level. Iron ore was extracted from the mine between 1902 and 1947, the workings extending under much of Drayton Park.

171 Former cottages for ironworkers
SP 989785 ★
On the south side of Kettering Road Islip, ¼ mile west of bridge over River Nene. *King William Cottages,* a terrace of 10 brick cottages was built in 1903 for workers at the Islip Iron Co.'s Ironworks, the latter operating from 1873 to 1942.

172 Former watermill
SP 991792 ★ LBII
On an arm of the River Nene, the former corn mill is at the end of Mill Road leading from the north end of Islip. A long two-storey stone building with several courses of brick below the eaves and at the top of the gable ends, indicating the present slate roof replaced one of thatch. The mill used to house two under-shot water-wheels. The mill house is at

right angles to the north-west end. Flour milling finished in 1960 but grinding of animal foods, using electricity, continued until about 1970. All buildings are now converted to dwellings.

KELMARSH   B3
173 Former twin railway tunnels
SP 752793 to SP 750797 ★
On Brampton Valley Way, the former trackbed of the LNWR's Northampton to Market Harborough line, about ½ mile south of the Kelmarsh to Arthingworth road crossing. Some 525yds (480m) long, the western bore of the tunnel dates from the opening of the line in 1859. The eastern bore was dug when the line was doubled in 1879 and contains a chimney vent. The portals are of blue brick. The line was closed to rail traffic in 1981 and the eastern bore is now open to pedestrians and cyclists as part of the linear park. A similar set of twin tunnels lies 2 miles further north at Great Oxendon (SP 738833).

170 Vent shaft for underground workings, Islip

KETTERING C3

From the mid-17thC, the manufacture of worsted cloth was Kettering's main industry. In 1778 however, Thomas Gotch started manufacturing boots and shoes adjacent to Chesham House in Lower St. By the 1850s when the worsted industry declined, boot & shoe manufacturing became the town's main industry. Spurred on by the arrival of the Midland Railway in 1857, the population expanded rapidly from 5,000 in 1851 to nearly 30,000 by 1901. At its height, there were more than 50 companies in the shoe and leather industries but the decline in the 2nd half of the 20thC has left only one or two.

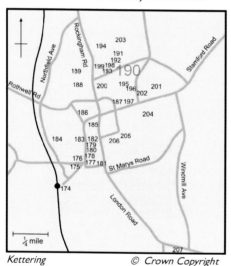

Kettering   © *Crown Copyright*

174 Kettering station
SP 864780 ★ LBII
On the Midland Main Line, the station is reached from the town centre via Station Rd. Opened in 1857 on the Midland Railway's Leicester to Hitchin extension, the station is noted for its decorated cast-iron pillars and supports for the ridged wrought-iron platform canopies. These were originally covered in glass, now modern plastic sheeting. The station was enlarged in 1879 when the line was quadrupled and the present brick and terracotta station building opened in 1895. The Midland Railway motif is notable on the road frontage.

175 Former ironstone company offices
SP 866783 ★ C
Northampton House, on Station Rd at its junction with Northampton Rd. JT Blackwell designed this 2-storey Edwardian building in brick with stone embellishments and a slate roof. It was built in 1910 as offices for James Pain, the iron ore magnate who had extensive ironstone quarries in north Northamptonshire during the 19thC and 20thC. The company still occupied Northampton House in 1927. An application was submitted to demolish the building in 2009 but it is currently occupied by a homecare agency.

176 Bus garage
SP 865783 ★
On the north side of Northampton Rd between the town centre and the railway. A plain building readily identifiable as being of its time i.e.1935. Charles Adams & Co. of Wellingborough erected it for United Counties Omnibus Co. at a cost of £16,000 to accommodate 100 buses. The garage continues in use by their successors today and remains essentially unaltered (see also Site 199).

177 Alfred East Art Gallery
SP 867783 ○ LBII C
In Sheep St to the south of the parish church. Built in 1913 to the design of local architect JA Gotch, the building is constructed in ashlar Weldon stone in the classical style and is, properly for an art gallery, windowless. The south elevation with its central, arched entrance, overlooks ornamental gardens whence access to Sheep Street is gained by an imposing flight of steps adjoining the gallery wall. Free access Tue-Sat. (www.kettering.gov.uk)

178 Dryland memorial fountain and horse troughs
SP 867783 ★ C
On the east side of Sheep St to the south of the parish church. The memorial was designed by JA Gotch and erected by public subscription in 1907 to the memory of Dr JW Dryland. It contained a drinking fountain, two horse troughs and a lower trough for dogs.

The horse troughs were removed in 1947 with the demise of horse transport, but replacements were unveiled in 1995.

179 Former Hippodrome cinema/ variety theatre
SP 867785 ★ C

On the east side of the Market Place. The building occupies a commanding position and is 2 (tall) storeys high, of brick and limestone construction arranged in three blind-arched bays. It was designed by FE Law of Northampton and built as the Corn Exchange and Town Hall, opening in 1854. Converted to *Vint's Electric Palace* in 1909, it had a floor plan measuring 58 x 32ft (18 x 10m), a gallery and the ability to present stage shows. The building passed into local hands in 1912 operating as *The Palace* and in 1917 changed names again to the *Hippodrome* (the painted sign is still visible on the south elevation), closing c1921. Now used as part café, part shop.

180 Manor House Museum
SP 867784 ○ LBII* C

Just south of the parish church, behind the library in Sheep St. Located in the former Manor House, the town's museum includes a range of industrial exhibits, for example boot and shoe making machinery and displays on local brickmaking and ironworking. Of particular interest is a car made by Robinson of Kettering. Free entry Tue-Sat. (www.kettering.gov.uk)

181 Former cattle market buildings
SP 868783 ★ C

At the junction of London Rd and Bowling Green Rd, a range of mainly single-storey buildings curves gracefully round the corner. It was built in 1880 of Northamptonshire sand ironstone with window surrounds in limestone. The array of structures – now offices – includes the former market keeper's house,

weighbridge office and refreshment room. At the west end, the former shed with clerestory roof housed the steam roller purchased in 1886 by the Urban District Council.

179 Former Hippodrome, Market Place, Kettering

182 Former fire station
SP 867786 ★ C

Off the north side of Market St. A two-storey building erected in 1926 as the town's fire station. The side facing Market St has two sets of large double doors. At second-storey level to the west of the double doors is a louvred rectangular opening possibly associated with hose drying. From the 1950s the building was used as the ambulance station but is now in other use.

183 Former Regal cinema
SP 866786 ★ C

On the west side of High St. Opened in 1936 as *The Regal*, this was Kettering's only purpose-built 'super cinema'. The front elevation boasts a central, glazed rotunda with two flanking wings in red brick. Total capacity was 1742 in stalls and circle. There was a sizeable mezzanine restaurant and stage shows were a regular feature. Renamed the *Granada* in 1948 it converted to a bingo hall in 1974.

184 Entrance to former gasworks
SP 863785 ★

On the north side of Meadow Road, just east of its junction with Jutland Way, ¼ mile west of the town centre. Originally above a doorway of the c1890 offices, a stone pediment with *Kettering Gas Co. Ltd.* beneath is set in the brick wall adjacent to the former entrance to the gasworks which existed on this site from 1834 to the 1960s.

185 Former telephone call office
SP 867788 ★ C

On the south side of Ebenezer Place, off Silver St. A 3-storey building of 6 bays in brick with stone embellishments including rustication at ground-floor level, built about the turn of the 20thC. This was the location of the National Telephone Company's Public Call Office, taken over by the General Post Office in 1912 and used as the telephone exchange until 1937.

186 Former malting for Elworthy brewery
SP 865789 ★

On the north-east side of Lower St, north-west of Tanners Lane. A four-storey brick building of 6 bays, the north-west half has a slated pyramid roof surmounted by a tall rectangular cowl for the kiln. A stone tablet on the west side has the date of 1904 and the initials JE for John Elworthy whose family had been brewers at the adjacent Crown Brewery since 1875 until a takeover by Marston, Thompson and Evershed of Burton-on-Trent in 1931. Brewing continued until 1940. Most of the brewery was demolished in 1964 but parts around the old brewery yard remain.

187 Former Empire cinema
SP 870790 ★

On the north side of Eskdaill St at the eastern edge of the town centre. The façade has a stuccoed central arch and two flanking bays. This was Kettering's 2nd purpose-built cinema, the first being the *Gaumont Pavilion* in High Street, demolished in 1960. *The Empire* opened in May 1920 with a seating capacity of 400, including a small balcony, popular with courting couples due to the provision of

186 Former Elworthy brewery maltings, Lower St, Kettering

double seats. It was operated throughout its existence by local people, closing as a cinema in 1954. It is now in use as a tyre depot.

188 Former shoe and clothing factories in Field St
SP 865792 ★

In Field St, at its junctions with Dryden St and Cobden St, ¼ mile north of the town centre. On the north-west corner of the Field St/Cobden St junction is a former 3-storey shoe factory dating from 1878, built of red brick with attractive white and blue brick facings for the round-headed windows and now converted to apartments. On the south-east corner of the Field St/Dryden St junction is the four-storey factory of the former Kettering Clothing Manufacturing Co-operative Society (Kaycee) built in 1895. The office block in Dryden St has a Venetian style porch. The early 20[th]C 4-storey buildings in brick and concrete on the south-west corner of the Field St/Cobden St junction have been refurbished and converted to apartments.

189 Former Glendon Engine Works
SP 864796 ★

At the west end of Sackville St, to the west of Rockingham Rd, ½ mile north of the town centre. The Glendon Engine Works were erected in the 1870s and operated by Jessop & Co. who in 1878 were described as 'manufacturers of locomotive and stationary engines and every description of engine pumps'. There was one large shop 100ft (30m) long, 40ft (12m) wide and 20ft (6m) high. The premises, with additions, are now occupied by Henry Billson Ltd., steel stockholders.

190 Streetscape of shoe & leather factories and housing in Regent St and Bath Rd area
SP 8779 ★

Between Rockingham Rd, Montagu St and Bath Rd, north-east of the town centre. From the 1880s a number of factories were constructed for shoe manufacturers and related suppliers, interspersed with terraced housing. The latter were generally built with single-storey workshops in the gardens, often used by shoe outworkers for stitching and attaching operations. Some of the key factory buildings in this area are described below (Sites 191-8).

191 Loake shoe factory
SP 869796 ★

On the north side of Wood St, between Wilson Terrace and Park Rd. Loake Shoemakers was founded in 1880 in Kettering and this factory was built for the company in 1894, being one of the earlier single-storey shoe

192 Motif on former Kettering Co-operative Boot & Shoe Manufacturing Society factory, Havelock St, Kettering

factories, with a 2-storey office frontage having shaped gables on three sides. It is one of the county's few shoe factories still in production under the same family name, manufacturing men's high quality welted footwear.

192 Former Kettering Co-operative Boot & Shoe Manufacturing Society factory
SP 868794 ★

On the north side of Havelock St, near its junction with Wellington St. Built in 1890, this is a 3-storey red brick building with corner oriel windows to 1st and 2nd storeys. Note the *Hand in Hand* motif in stone below the oriel window on the first floor. KCB&SMS later moved to a new factory further down Havelock St (now demolished). The factory is now converted to apartments but the white window frames are disappointing.

193 Former Hales & Jowett shoe factory
SP 868793 ★ LBII

On the north side of Regent St. Built in 1890 and used initially by Hales & Jowett, this 3-storey factory has an 8-bay symmetrical frontage, with large iron windows having iron mullions. It is now a bedding showroom.

194 Former Hulett shoe factory
SP 868796 ★

On the north side of William St, this small, three-storey, former shoe factory is now converted to apartments. The wall-mounted crane remains on the west gable end.

195 Former Gravestock & Wright shoe factory
SP 871792 ★

On the east side of Tresham St is a 3-storey shoe factory of 25 bays, dating from 1894 built for Gravestock & Wright and taken over by George Wright when the partnership was dissolved in 1914. Converted to apartments.

196 Former T Bird shoe factory
SP 872792 ★ LBII

Globe Works at the Bath Rd/Digby St junction off Stamford Rd. This three-storey brick-built factory has mainly iron-framed windows with stone embellishments and oriel windows on the corner at first and second storeys. It was built for Thomas Bird after his partnership with George Abbott dissolved in 1891 (see Site 206) and this business lasted well into the 20thC. Part of the building is still in use by EA Tailby, heel manufacturer.

197 Former FS Bryant leather dressing factory
SP 871790 ★

On the north side of Montagu St at its junction with Wellington St. On a large corner plot, this three-storey factory plus basement was first used by Henry Hanger, a boot & shoe manufacturer. A datestone over the side entrance shows 1887. For several decades in the 20thC it was FS Bryant leather dressers; more recently a furniture showroom. Of red brick, with banded stonework and with an oriel window on the truncated corner at first floor level above the main entrance. It is now converted to apartments.

198 Former shoe factory, Havelock St
SP 867793 ★ LBII

Built on the rear gardens of 4 & 6 Havelock St, accessed from an alleyway between No.4 Havelock St and Site 199. A three-storey shoe factory with L-shaped plan constructed between 1860 and 1884. It is much larger than the typical shoeworkers' garden workshops, but smaller than the majority of shoe factory buildings in this area. In 1929 it was Clipstone & Whitwell's leather lace factory but is now used for other purposes.

199 Former bus garage
SP 867793 ★

On the south side of Havelock St, 100yds from its junction with Rockingham Rd. This narrow-fronted but deep building was erected by the United Counties Omnibus Co. in 1922 to hold a mere ten buses. Designed by Talbot, Brown & Fisher of Wellingborough, it was built by Smith, Edmunds & Co., whose base was also in Havelock St, at a cost of £3,100. This building was sold by UCOC when the company's Northampton Rd garage came into use in 1935 (see Site 176).

200 Former Co-op bakery
SP 868792 ★

Situated on the west side of Crown St between Regent St and King St, off Rockingham Rd, the Co-operative Model Bakery was constructed in 1900. It is a red brick building of three storeys and 8 bays with stone banding on pilasters between bays at 1st and 2nd storeys. Between each storey are elaborate cast-iron tie-plates formed from the initials *KICS* (Kettering Industrial Co-operative Society). The building has been converted to apartments with sympathetic replacement windows. The north end of the building is adjacent to the former KICS grocery warehouse, fronting on to Regent St.

200 Former Co-op bakery, Crown St ,Kettering

201 Wicksteed engineering works
SP 873792 ★

Between Digby St and Bath Lane, with Lawson St on its east side ½ mile east of the town centre. The company was started in 1876 by Charles Wicksteed to make steam ploughing equipment and simple machine tools. At one time there was an elaborate entrance arch to the premises but this was demolished some 30 years ago. The land slopes down westwards from Lawson Street so that there is a marked difference between the height of the walls at each end. The firm, now Wicksteed Leisure, focuses on playground and similar leisure equipment.

202 Timson Perfecta engineering works
SP 872791 ★

In Bath Rd and Catesby St, off Montagu St. The firm of Timson, Bullock and Barber moved in 1903 to the Perfecta Works in Catesby St and in 1916 erected offices in Bath Rd, backing on to the Catesby St works. The following year they built an additional workshop opposite their offices in Bath Rd. In 1933 the firm's name was changed to Timsons Ltd. by which time production focused on printing machinery. The former Methodist Chapel in Bath Rd, opposite the 1916 offices, was purchased and converted to offices. Most of the original buildings were demolished during the 1980s and 1990s to be replaced by well-styled modern brick buildings, with an impressive multi-storey, multi-sided block at the corner of Bath Rd and Montagu St. Of the older buildings, the converted chapel and 1916 offices are prominent survivors.

203 Bandstand in Rockingham Rd Park
SP 868797 ★

Reached via Charles St off Rockingham Rd, ½ mile north of the town centre. The bandstand has an octagonal brick and concrete base surmounted by an ogee-section segmented roof with a slightly extended canopy, supported on cast-iron columns. The boarded ceiling is held in place by a multitude of iron bands.

204 Timson foundry
SP 873789 ★

On the east side of Water St a short distance south from Montagu St, ½ mile east of the town centre, is the site of the foundry taken over by Timson, Bullock & Barber in 1927. Their successors, Timson Ltd., erected a large machine shop alongside and in the late 1990s redeveloped the foundry. It is now the only working iron foundry in the county.

205 Former Newman shoe factory
SP 871786 ★ LBII

In Newman St off Mill Rd, east of the town centre. Built for N Newman & Sons in the 1870s, this shoe factory is of Italianate appearance in red brick with stone dressings. There is a three-storey C-shaped range, with addit-

ional single-storey structures on either side of the main spine. The 7-bay frontage on the north side has a 4-storey central tower which used to have a pyramidal roof. In the 1930s, it was used by G Essam & Co. Today it is used by bespoke shoemakers Ken Hall Shoes.

206 Former Abbott & Bird shoe factory
SP 869786 ★ LBII

In Green Lane off Horsemarket, on the eastern side of the town centre. This impressive three-storey factory was built in 1873 for Abbott & Bird. By 1891 the partnership had dissolved (see Site 196) and the building has since had a variety of uses. It is of red brick, with stone arches over round-headed windows, stone quoins and stringers. The roof has elaborately corbelled eaves. It was the first factory to be constructed of bricks produced by the Kettering Brick & Tile Co.

206 Former Abbott & Bird shoe factory, Green Lane, Kettering

207 Wicksteed Park
SP 880773 ○

One mile south of the town centre, off Barton Rd. The 150-acre Wicksteed Park opened in 1920, the brainchild of Charles Wicksteed (1847-1931). The lakeside railway, with station, bridges and a tunnel, has operated since 1931, the two original steam outline petrol-engined locomotives have been replaced by steam outline diesels but are still used occasionally. In addition the park boasts a central pavilion, rose gardens, boating lake and playgrounds. The former cycle track and the cinema have changed use over the years but can still be identified. Free access to pedestrians in daylight hours. (www.wicksteedpark.co.uk)

KILSBY   A3

208 Kilsby Tunnel
SP 565714 to SP 579697 ★ LBII*

208 North portal of Kilsby tunnel

The north portal (SP 565714) is immediately to the east side of the railway bridge carrying the A5 over the West Coast Main Line about ¼ mile north of Kilsby village. A ventilation shaft (SP 569709) can be seen on the north side of the A5, about ½ mile east of Kilsby village. The south portal (SP 579697) is adjacent to the minor road from Crick to Ashby St. Ledgers, ½ mile south of the staggered junction with the A5. Kilsby tunnel was a major feature in the building of the London & Birmingham Railway. It is 1½ miles long and opened in 1838 after problems with flooding and rioting navvies. The two portals are of dressed stone. The 60ft (18m) diameter ventilation shaft is one of two, being of brick construction with castellated decoration (the other is visible from the M45). Additional smaller shafts and spoil heaps outline the course of the tunnel on the surface.

209 Disused section of Watling Street
SP 579713 – SP 571729 ★
Extending NNW and SSE of the byway from Kilsby to Crick, between the LNWR's Northampton to Rugby line and the M1 motorway. Surprisingly substantial earthworks mark the course of the London to Holyhead road prior to its 19thC realignment. At the northern end, the modern Daventry International Railfreight Terminal gives a stark contrast between 'old and discarded' and 'new and thriving'.

KING'S CLIFFE   D4

210 Former Eagle brewery
TL 004972 ★ C
At the corner of West St and Eagle Lane, part of the former Eagle Brewery is now occupied by the Old Brewery Studio. The Cunnington family were associated with brewing in King's Cliffe from the first half of the 19thC. The Ketton & King's Cliffe Brewery Company was at the brewery from 1898 until 1900. From 1901 the business was conducted as the Malt and Hop Company, first by G K Papillon as proprietor and from 1910 by Charles Campbell McLeod until it closed in 1919.

211 Former watermill
TL 007970 ★ LBII C
On the Willow Brook, at the end of a lane heading south by the church. A three-storey corn mill of stone with a stone slate roof, the north-east corner of the walls is deeply chamfered and curves out from some way above the first floor to become a normal corner about 6ft (2m) below the eaves. In the 17thC there were two water-wheels here, later a single wheel was used until sometime before WWI. The mill has been cleared of all machinery and is converted to a dwelling.

212 Former fire engine house
TL 007971 ★ LBII C
Situated on the west side of Hall Yard, near the church. The single-storey building of stone, with a Collyweston slate roof, has dressed quoins to the north gable end with wide double wooden doors, once red but now painted green. On the side is marked *Erected by subscription 1831*.

212 Former fire engine house, King's Cliffe

213 Former King's Cliffe station house
TL 009976 ★
In Station Rd, King's Cliffe, off the King's Cliffe to Wansford road, about ¼ mile north of the centre of the village. The brick-built station house is all that remains of King's Cliffe station on the former LNWR's Seaton to Wansford line, opened in 1879 and closed in 1966.

214 Wall-mounted AA village sign
TL 008974 ★
On the wall of the former *Old Red Lion* on the north side of Park St. A circular enamelled AA village sign for King's Cliffe, yellow with black lettering, dating from pre-1922 and indicating distances in miles to: *Kettering (15), Stamford (7) and London (87½).*

KING'S SUTTON   A1
215 Former Twyford watermill
SP 487373 ❑
On the River Cherwell, north of the bridge for the King's Sutton to East Adderbury road. Known as Twyford Mill to distinguish it from another mill in King's Sutton, this former corn mill is a four-storey brick building with, at its east end, a projection downstream. One bay from the west end, a tower rises some distance above the ridge of the slate roof to support a rectangular water tank. By 1906 a roller-milling plant had been installed as had an Armfield water turbine and a steam engine.

Flour milling seems to have ceased in the 1930s and the mill, together with later industrial buildings adjacent to it, is now used for other purposes.

KISLINGBURY   B2
216 Former watermill
SP 694594 ★ C
On the south side of the River Nene and approached by Mill Rd heading west from the centre of the village. The three-storey brick mill with slate roof and round-headed cast-iron windows has on its north-west side an earlier two-storey stone building which might be the mill built in 1642 by the Rector of Kislingbury. The buildings are now used for fireplace manufacture.

LAMPORT   B3
217 Former Lamport station
SP 751752 ★
Adjacent to Brampton Valley Way, the former trackbed of the LNWR's Northampton to Market Harborough line, adjacent to where it crosses the A508 between Lamport and Maidwell. Opened in 1859 it is the only surviving station building on the branch. It has decorated stone gables and is rendered, as it was in operating days. The station closed to passengers in 1960.

218 Former ironstone tramway tunnel
SP 753729 ★
On the A508, immediately south of its junction with the minor road to Scaldwell. Brick parapets remain on either side of the road where Staveley Coal & Iron Co.'s standard gauge tramway passed beneath the road carrying iron ore from the Lamport Quarries on the east side of the A508 down to calcine clamps adjacent to the LNWR's Northampton to Market Harborough line. The bridge which dates from WW2 was used until 1963. In the field on the west side of the A508, the apex of the tunnel arch can just be seen. Immediately north of the road junction was the point at which the Company's earlier aerial ropeway crossed the road, carrying iron ore from Scaldwell down to the railway (see Site 367).

LITTLE HARROWDEN   C3

219 Former cottages for ironworkers
SP 894721 ★
Immediately to the west of the Midland Main Line in Furnace Lane. Best approached from Finedon Station Rd, 1½ miles north-west of Finedon. Three terraces of cottages were built for workers at the adjacent Finedon Furnaces owned by the Glendon Iron Ore Co. and operated from 1866 until 1891. The most notable is the terrace of 9 brick-built cottages furthest from the railway. They have windows with pointed arches lined in polychrome brick.

LODDINGTON   C3

220 Former cottages for ironstone workers
SP 817783 ★
On the south side of Harrington Rd, ¼ mile from its junction with Cransley Rd. A terrace of 12 brick cottages named *Ellistown* was built in 1904 by Loddington Ironstone Co. to house some of its workers who were employed at the nearby quarries.

LONG BUCKBY   A2

221 Former Castle shoe factory
SP 626676 ★
On the north side of King St to the west of the Market Square. The main three-storey shoe factory was built by Alfred Howe by 1884, although the building on its left may date from c1870. Used as a shoe factory until the early 1990s, it is now converted to offices but retains the original windows.

222 Former shoe outworkers' workshops
SP 635677 ★ LBII
Located behind Nos. 45 to 53 East St, these two-storey brick-built workshops were constructed in the mid-19thC for use by shoe outworkers. Note the large windows in the upper storey. There are a number of other examples in the town, both single and two storey, for example behind houses in Church St and King St.

223 Former gasworks house
SP 623678 ★
Situated on the north side of West St opposite its junction with Parkfield Road. The white rendered brick building with slate roof carries a datestone of 1898 and was the former manager's house on the gas works site of the Long Buckby Gas-Light, Coke and Coal Co. Ltd., established in 1860. The company was taken over by the Northampton Gas-Light Co. in 1933. Some 250yds further west on the north side of the road just past the sign for Murcott (SP 621679) is the stub of a former cast-iron lamp-post set into the stone wall. It carries the words *LONG BUCKBY GAS* cast into its side.

224 Former Upper Murcott watermill
SP 622678 ★
Served by Nenmoor stream, a tributary of the River Nene, this corn mill stands on the south side of West St at the eastern end of the town. The brick two-storey building with a slate roof was at one time thatched. In 1857 it was described as having a 20ft (6m) diameter water-wheel driving three pairs of stones and had a 10 horsepower condensing engine by Wood & Son, Leeds. The steam engine went out of use at the time of WWI and the water-wheel by WW2 although an oil engine was used for gristing until the early 1960s. The mill is now a dwelling called *Willow Mill*.

222 Former shoe outworkers' workshops, Long Buckby

of 17ft (5.2m). At the side of each can be seen the remains of side-ponds built in 1805 to save water, and used until 1929 when back-pumping was introduced. Until 1914, Lock No.9 was a gauging lock, where boats were gauged in order to calculate the weight of cargo they were carrying. For the other locks in the flight see under Norton and Whilton. Approximately 100yds north of lock No.9 is a cast-iron milepost (LBII) with the inscription: *G/CCo Braunston 5 miles.*

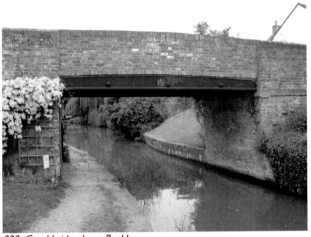

228 Canal bridge, Long Buckby

225 Former water-wheel pump
SP 623679 ★
Relocated to an open-fronted shed in the Nature Reserve on the north side of West St nearly opposite Upper Murcott mill, this small overshot water-wheel and pump was moved from Foxhill Court, between Long Buckby and West Haddon, in 1990.

226 Canal settlement
SP 612654 ★ C
Buckby Wharf is about 1¾ miles from the centre of the main village on the road to Daventry. With the development of traffic on the Grand Union Canal it had at various times brickworks, maltings, a brewery, a rope walk and a public house. Although these have either been demolished or converted to dwellings, the canal's influence on the growth of this outpost of the main village may still be detected.

227 Canal locks
SP 611655 - 614652 ★ C
Lock Nos. 8 and 9 are part of the Whilton and Buckby flight on the Grand Union Canal, built in 1796. Lock No. 8 is reached by walking north along the tow-path from the road connecting Long Buckby to the A5. Lock No. 9 is reached by walking south from the same point. These two wide locks have a total fall

228 Canal bridge with cast-iron beams
SP 608655 ★ LBII C
Over the Grand Union Canal about 300yds south-east of its bridge beneath the A5. Bridge No. 12 is an early 19thC brick accommodation bridge with cambered cast-iron beams on stone supports, carrying 4 shallow, brick barrel vaults supporting the roadway.

LOWICK D3
229 Remains of transfer sidings in Marsh's Pit
SP 973799 ❏
The Islip Iron Co. had extensive workings in the vicinity of Islip, Lowick, Slipton, Sudborough and Twywell between 1877 and 1952. Marsh's Pit is in a remote spot to the west of the former 3ft (0.91m) gauge tramway route which ran from quarries at Sudborough in the north down to the furnaces at Islip. It is about ½ mile south of the former level crossing on the Lowick to Drayton road (SP 974807). At the far west end of Marsh's Pit is the former adit into Church Mine North, now blocked, part of the extensive underground workings beneath Drayton Park (see also Site 170). Adjacent to the adit are remains of sidings used to transfer ore from 2ft.6in (0.76m) gauge mine wagons to 3ft (0.91m) gauge wagons for transit to the furnaces. They are

very difficult to find in summer when undergrowth makes Marsh's Pit all but impenetrable.

230 Earthworks at Slipton
SP 951793 ★

On the eastern side of the hamlet of Slipton in Lowick parish, the land falls away sharply behind the houses, evidence of ironstone quarrying which took place between 1877 and c1900. Platforms remain in places where houses and gardens once stood.

229 Remains of transfer sidings in Marsh's Pit, Lowick

231 Tunnels for former
tramway at Slipton
SP 950797 ★

In Lowick parish, ½ mile north of Slipton on the road to Sudborough. Two former tramway tunnels remain beneath the road, each about 100ft (30m) long, 6ft (2m) in diameter, lined with brick. The southern tunnel served North Pattins Quarry, the remains of which are to the west of the road. This is now used as a culvert. The northern tunnel served Willow Close Mine and is blocked at its western end. There are remains of transfer sidings adjacent to the eastern portal but access is difficult in summer due to undergrowth.

232 Spring head
SP 973806 ★

On the south side of the road from Lowick to Drayton House, opposite Mordant Close, is a stone surround and trough for a still flowing outlet from a spring. The stonework carries the date 1830.

MILTON MALSOR   B2

233 Former Hope Brewery
SP 733557 ★ C

Situated to the east of the old Northampton to Towcester road, the former Hope Brewery is just north of the *Greyhound* pub. The part next to the pub was built in 1879 by William John East to replace an earlier brewhouse on the site. It is of three storeys with a slate ridge roof. Adjoining it on the north is a taller three-storey brick building of three bays, red brick with a three-brick wide string course of lighter coloured brick between each storey. This extension to the brewery was built in 1888 and was the only brewery in Northamptonshire to be described in Alfred Barnard's *The Noted Breweries of Great Britain and Ireland* published 1889-1891. The brewery was taken over by the Northampton Brewery Company in 1904 and the brewing plant sold. The buildings have been converted to offices.

NASEBY   B3

234 Former brewhouse
SP 688782 ★

On the west of Church St, opposite the junction with the road to Clipston, the *Fitzgerald Arms* has the shell of a former brewhouse at the rear, almost completely surrounded by other buildings. It now houses the toilets.

235 Naseby canal reservoir
SP 667780 ★

Immediately south-east of the junction between the A5199 and the A14. Constructed for the Leicester line of the Grand Union Canal, Naseby Reservoir came into use in 1821. Supplied from the River Avon at the east end, and a brook at the south, the dam is on the north side parallel to and about 300yds to the south of the A14. A four mile long feed along another brook leads to the end of the Welford branch of the canal.

NETHER HEYFORD   B2
236 Remains of Heyford Ironworks
SP 654578 ★
In a field immediately to the south-east of Furnace Lane (the road from Nether Heyford to Upper Stowe), between the canal and railway bridges. Heyford Ironworks operated from 1857-1891, initially by George Pell & Co. and from 1873 by the Heyford Iron Co. Ltd. The hearths of three blast furnaces remain to a height of 6-10ft (2-3m) and were visible for many years but have now been covered by an earth bund. Surviving structures are the works office now a domestic building, and stables associated with the tramway system. The adjacent railway embankment retaining wall contains refractory brick and slag.

237 Former Stowe Quarries tramway embankment
SP 647578 to SP 650579 ★
On a footpath running from the A5 Watling Street near its junction with the road to Church Stowe, under the West Coast Main Line and thence to Furnace Lane in Nether Heyford. A well-preserved standard gauge tramway embankment overlays an earlier narrow gauge track. It was built to carry ironstone from Stowe-Nine-Churches quarries to Stowe Ironworks adjacent to the railway and later to a connection with the LNWR itself. It operated from 1863 to 1878 and then carried limestone until dismantled in 1920.

238 Disused part of Watling Street
SP 647578 ★
Not so immediately apparent as other abandoned sections of Watling Street in the county but worth seeking out nonetheless. The easiest viewing point is from the footpath leading ENE from the A5, opposite the junction with the minor road to Church Stowe. From a point about 50 yards along this path, look south-west along a line parallel with the present A5 and wait for the old hedgeline, flat top and earthworks of the old alignment to spring from the countryside!

NEWNHAM   A2
239 Former windmill
SP 576609 ★ LBII
On the west side of the lane heading north from the village to Daventry. A brick tower mill built about 1820 for milling corn, three storeys high, carrying four sails driving two pairs of stones and a dressing machine. It was abandoned during the latter part of the 19thC. After use as an observation tower before WWI it became derelict and crumbled away from the top. The structure was repaired and the viewing gallery and new roof were installed in 1990.

240 Remains of water pump
SP 581598 ★
On the west side of the B4037 as it approaches the church from the north. A cast-iron pump, fluted at the top and on the cap, marked with the symbol of a lion, still with handle although no longer connected to the water supply.

239 Former windmill, Newnham

NORTHAMPTON B2

During the 16thC the major trade in Northampton changed from woollens to shoemaking. By 1725 the town had gained its national reputation for producing boots and shoes and this remained the major industry until the mid-20thC. From 1742 until about 1760, the world's first water-powered cotton spinning mill operated in the town but nothing survives of this. Because of the topography, the main lines of both canal and railway missed the town but after the branch canal opened in 1815 there was increased activity in the iron-working trades and brewing. The boot & shoe and other manufacturing industr-

ies have declined since WW2 to be replaced by developments in the service industries.

NORTHAMPTON - CENTRAL

241 Central Museum and Art Gallery
SP 756604 ○ C
On the west side of Guildhall Rd. The museum houses the National Shoe Collection but also has many exhibits relating to the manufacture of footwear. There are a vast number of machines in the reserve collection. The upper floor displays on the history of Northampton have many references to industry, including a reconstruction of a shoe-

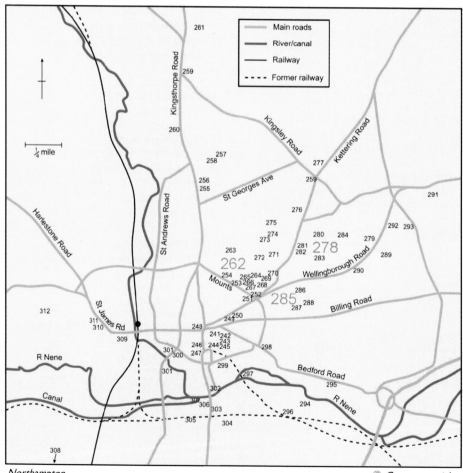

Northampton © *Crown copyright*

worker's home and items on brickmaking and foundry work. Free access Tue-Sun. (www.northampton.gov.uk/museums)

242 Royal Theatre
SP 756603 ○ LBII C

On the east side of Guildhall Rd. Despite its cramped frontage, this building designed by CJ Phipps and built in 1887 is a splendid example of Victorian theatre architecture. Approximately 550 seats in stalls, circle, boxes and gallery give (mostly) good views of the stage through the tall proscenium arch. There is also a superb *Sipario Dipinto* (decorated safety curtain) by the late local artist Henry Bird. The auditorium has rich plasterwork decoration to the fronts of circle, gallery and boxes and massive pillars frame the boxes. The paint shop, visible from Derngate, standing between the Royal Theatre's and Derngate concert hall's rear entrances, pre-dates both and was purpose-built to paint scenery on a jobbing basis.

243 Façade of former Phipps & Son Ltd. shoe mercery
SP 756603 ★ C

On the east side of Guildhall Rd, immediately below the Royal Theatre. Now part of the Royal & Derngate theatre complex, the façade of the former shoe mercers Phipps & Son Ltd. has been retained, five storeys high with multi-coloured brickwork. Phipps were one of the largest suppliers of components to the shoe industry for many years from the late 19thC.

244 Former Vulcan engineering works
SP 756603 ★ LBII C

On the west side of Guildhall Rd, between Angel Lane and St. John's St, is the façade of the former Vulcan works. It has two storeys and nine bays mainly of bricks with large semi-circular topped windows for the first floor. The first storey of the third bay from the north end has large double doors with cast-

iron bollards each side to protect the walls at either side of the entrance from being damaged by wagon or cart wheels. The Vulcan works were started in 1877 by Henry Mobbs to complement his Lion Foundry which he had purchased in 1868. Later Phipps & Son Ltd., shoe mercers, took over the Vulcan works. The premises are now used by a number of different businesses.

245 Façade of former CWS saleroom
SP 756603 ★ C

On the east side of Guildhall Rd, extending between Angel Lane and St. John's St. A Cooperative Wholesale Society saleroom was first opened on this site in October 1890 but the present buildings are of later date. At the southern end is a four-storey brick façade carrying a date of 1921, the rest of the building having been demolished to build apartments. It is embellished with characteristic moulded CWS wheatsheaf surrounded by more decorative brick in the gables, over a mock rusticated stone basement storey. The art-deco style building at the northern end (LBII) was constructed in 1936, the entrance on the corner with Angel Lane having an impressive circular staircase.

243 Former Phipps shoe mercery, Guildhall Rd, Northampton

246 Former premises of Bassett-Lowke, model engineers
SP 754603 ★

On the east side of Kingswell St and facing south down it on the bend, is a four-storey yellow brick building with red brick surrounds to windows and doors and a slight hipped slate roof. It has three bays on the side facing south, one bay at 45 degrees to this and one bay facing west. Originally used as a cabinet factory, in 1910 it became the head office of Bassett-Lowke Ltd, model engineers. It was vacated by the company in 1931 and has been used for a variety of purposes since.

247 Former Albion Steam Brewery
SP 754602 ★

Situated between Commercial St and Foundry St at the Kingswell St end, only a few buildings remain from the Albion Steam Brewery built in 1883 by Ratliffe and Jeffery, replacing smaller premises where Thomas Ratliffe started brewing in 1862. In Commercial St a modern building now stands on the site of the brewery warehouse but the 4-storey brewhouse remains attached to its east end and the former cooperage building faces onto Kingswell St next to the *King Billy* pub. The brewery was taken over by P Phipps & Co. Ltd. in 1899 and brewing ceased about 1903.

248 Former Phipps brewery offices
SP 754604 ★ LBII C

Number 8 on the north side of Gold Street was built in 1881 to the design of SJ Newman for the offices of P Phipps & Co. Ltd. It is three bays long, of brick and stone, three storeys plus an attic storey presenting a shaped gable onto Gold Street. The style is mixed 17thC Dutch and French.

249 Former M Inglis & Co. leather factors building
SP 756605 ★ LBII C

At the junction of Fish St and The Ridings. This is an imposing 5-storey building in stone and brick, designed by AE Anderson and built in 1901 for Malcolm Inglis and Co. of Glasgow, leather factors. The stonework is embellished with bulls' heads, shields and other motifs. The building is now converted to offices and a pub.

250 Façade of former Northampton Co-operative Society store
SP 757606 ★

On the south side of Abington St. Remodelling of Northampton Co-op Society's very large site in the middle of the town's principal shopping thoroughfare started in 1937, resulting in the impressive tiled, art-deco frontage to Abington St and the long arcade stretching through to St. Giles St. The almost perfectly symmetrical concave elevation has been amended but not drastically altered over the intervening years.

251 Former British United Shoe Machinery Co. depot
SP 759607 ★

At the south-west corner of the junction of Abington St and Lower Mounts. This three-storey office block with decorated gables was built in the 1890s for the International Goodyear Shoe Machinery Co. which became British United Shoe Machinery Co. in 1899. In the second half of the 20thC it became headquarters of the Northampton Town & County

247 Former brewhouse, Albion Steam Brewery, Commercial St, Northampton

(now Nationwide) Building Society. Since 1982 it has been home to BBC Radio Northampton.

252 Former Savoy cinema
SP 759608 ★ LBII

At the north-east corner of the junction of Abington St and Lower Mounts. Opened in 1936, the *Savoy* was arguably Northampton's principal cinema until its closure in 1995. Its frontage has an imposing stuccoed entrance diagonally across the corner. The south and west elevations host a variety of retail shops in dark red brick relieved by two stuccoed string courses. Designed by William R Glen, the auditorium originally held 1,954 people. Stage shows were readily accommodated, even after the auditorium was split into three mini-cinemas in 1974. In 1986 a full-blown cinema organ was re-introduced to replace the original Compton instrument destroyed by over-enthusiastic Cliff Richard fans in 1960! Renamed in turn: *ABC, EMI* and finally *Cannon*, the building is now *The Jesus Centre*.

NORTHAMPTON – NORTH
253 Former British United Shoe Machinery Co. factory
SP 757609 ★

On the north-west side of the junction of Upper Mounts and Earl St at the northern edge of the town centre. The three-storey brick-built premises was constructed c1923 for the British United Shoe Machinery Co. Initially used to manufacture tacks and other grindery, it was later used as a machinery repair factory. It was more recently used by Church's Shoes when the original very large windows were reduced in size but is now the *Charles Bradlaugh* bar-restaurant.

254 Fire station
SP 756609 ★

On the north side of Upper Mounts. Opened in 1935, this five-storey building of 16 bays frontage is flat-roofed with no decoration except between the windows of the top storey. The main part of the ground floor

256 Former Barratt Footshape Boot Works, Kingsthorpe Rd, Northampton

frontage is taken by the doors for the fire appliances.

255 Telegraph/ telephone cable junction marker
SP 753618 ★ C

On the east side of Kingsthorpe Rd, against the garden wall of 8 Elysium Terrace, ¾ mile north of the town centre. A cast-iron plate, originally installed to show the depth below the pavement of the junction in the telegraph line. It is 18in (46cm) high, approx 1½in (4cm) thick and 8in (20cm) wide for most of its height, with quarter-circle cut-outs at the top corners. A crown with the letters 'G' and 'R' on either side are cast on the face, with: 'ft in' below this, alongside which the figures for the depth would be painted, these having now worn off. See also Site 397.

256 Former Barratt Footshape Boot Works
SP 753619 ★ LBII C

On the east side of Kingsthorpe Rd, ¾ mile north of the town centre. This impressive three-storey frontage of 8 bays is the remains of a once extensive shoe factory designed by AE Anderson for the Barratt family. It is of red brick with elaborate terracotta embellishment. Mouldings within the two central semi-circular gables confirm the company was established in 1903 and the premises built in 1913. Stone lettering forms a balustrade at the eaves level proclaiming: *FOOTSHAPE BOOT WORKS*. The factory was taken over by Stylo in 1961 and finally closed c1998. The building is now in other use.

257 Façade of former George Webb 'Mentone' shoe factory
SP 755622 ★

In Bunting Rd and Brockton St, off Kingsthorpe Rd, about one mile north of the town centre. There was a shoe factory on this site from 1896 but it was rebuilt prior to George Webb taking over the site in 1927. Only the external walls of the later factory building remain, including an impressive façade with shaped gables in

257 Façade of former George Webb shoe factory, Bunting Rd, Northampton

Bunting Rd. George Webb were taken over by the Ward-White group in the 1960s and the shoe factory closed in 1982. It was subsequently used by a variety of small companies until the site was converted to apartments, the ornamental frontages being retained.

258 Former Miller Last Works
SP 755621 ★ LBII

On the corner of Arthur St and Bunting Rd, off Kingsthorpe Rd, about 1 mile north of the town centre. The two-storey plus basement factory was built in 1896 with extensions dated 1903 and 1923. It was owned by The Miller Last Company, an American company which manufactured shoemaking lasts. It is now the premises of Rushton Ablett who produce moulded footwear.

259 Former tram waiting shelters
SP 752629 ★

At the junction of Kingsthorpe Rd and Kingsthorpe Grove, opposite the *Cock Hotel*, 1 mile north of the town centre.

SP 765619 ★ C

At the junction of Kettering Rd and Kingsley Rd, opposite the *White Elephant* public house, 1 mile north-east of the town centre.

Two of Northampton's cast-iron tram waiting shelters survive, though not sited where they are of use to modern day bus passengers. With rounded ends, roof vents and decorative roof edgings they were both refurbished in the early 1990s.

260 Former tram cable duct inspection cover
SP 751625 ★

On Queen's Park Parade (Kingsthorpe Rd) in the footpath outside Grose's Vauxhall dealership, 1 mile north of the town centre. A survival of the tramway era is a Northampton Corporation Tramways inspection cover, complete with *NCT* lettering. This gave access to the feeder cable conduit and must have found a new use which justifies its retention.

261 Former Enterprise shoe factory
SP 753635 ★ LBII

On the south side of Bective Rd opposite its junction with Newington Rd, off Harborough Rd about 2 miles north of the town centre. Shoe factory built for Abraham Lee shortly after 1900 consisting of a range of single-storey north-lit sheds, fronted by a decorative façade with central arched entrance. Above the entrance is a gable attic with Venetian window, each side of which are a pair of consoles with *LB* in pierced stonework, probably for Lee Brothers. Attached to the east side is a later two-storey range c1924. The firm was still on this site in 1954 but the factory is now used by Expert Developments.

262 Streetscape of former shoe & leather factories and housing between Barrack Rd & Kettering Rd

North of The Mounts, bounded between Barrack Rd, Kettering Rd and the Racecourse. A streetscape of small to medium sized factory buildings constructed for boot & shoe manufacturers as well as suppliers to the leather and footwear trades, interspersed among streets of Victorian terraced housing. Key sites are outlined below (sites 263-275).

263 Former 6-storey Church's Shoes factory
SP 756612 ★

On the north side of Duke St about ½ mile north of the town centre. An impressive six-storey shoe factory, built at the end of the 19thC for Church's Shoes who occupied it until 1957 when the firm moved to St. James (Site 310). The ground floor frontage is of glazed brick. Now converted to apartments under the name *Church's Factory.*

264 Former Globe Leather Works
SP 758609 ★ LBII

Near the west end of Dunster St on its south side. An attractive brick-built factory, dating from c1890, 3 storeys plus basement, it has three gable ends facing onto the road in a Dutch style, the central one being decorated with pilasters and a shaped gable. Internally iron columns and joists support the floors. For over 50 years from the late 19thC, it was occupied by leather currier James Collier.

265 Former W Collier leather dressing factory
SP 758609 ★ LBII

On the north-east corner of the Overstone Rd / Dunster St junction. This 3-storey building dates from the 1870s. Its top storey has large wooden window frames which would

have originally contained wooden louvres to facilitate ventilation for the leather finishing processes. It is now converted to apartments.

266 Former GT Hawkins shoe factory
SP 758609 ★ LBII

Fronting Overstone Rd between Dunster St and St Michael's Rd is a range of 3-storey plus basement shoe factory buildings. The block on the corner of Overstone Rd and St Michaels Rd dates from c1875 and was originally the factory of Hornby & West. The factory on the Dunster St corner is from the late 1880s and was the original GT Hawkins factory. During the 2nd decade of the 20thC the whole building was taken over by GT Hawkins. Mid-way along the Overstone Rd frontage the trade name *Waukertz Shoes* is moulded in stone over the pedimented entrance. Hawkins, who were famous for their walking boots, ceased production in the 1990s and the premises remain vacant.

265 Former W Collier leather dressing factory, Overstone Rd, Northampton

267 Former Unicorn Works shoe factory
SP 758608 ★ LBII

On the south side of St Michaels Rd at Nos. 20-26. A shoe factory of 3 storeys and 10 bays, constructed c1890. Each end of the front elevation has an entrance on the ground floor and taking-in doors on the top floor with a wall mounted crane to the outer edge, suggesting the building was intended as two separate units.

268 RE Tricker shoe factory, St Michael's Rd, Northampton

268 RE Tricker shoe factory
SP 760609 ★ LBII
On the south side of St Michael's Rd at No. 56, is the brown glazed-tile frontage dating from 1937 of RE Tricker, having been manufacturing on the site since 1902. Originally a 2-storey factory, the third floor was added later. Used in the 2005 feature film *Kinky Boots* (see also Site 109). Next door at No. 62, Tricker has taken over the 3-storey premises that was formerly the shoe factory of Pollard & Sons.

269 Former HJ Bateman shoe factory
SP 761609 ★
On the north side of St Michael's Rd close to the Kettering Rd end. The 3-storey former shoe factory was built c1890 for HJ Bateman, later used by Northampton Machinery Co. before their move to Kingsthorpe Hollow in 1937 and is now Chaplin's Stage School. The remains of a crane hoist can still be seen above the loading doors on the frontage.

270 Gateway to Dickens leather factory
SP 762610 ★
On the west side of Kettering Rd, between its junctions with St Michael's Rd and Grove Rd. A narrow, arched gateway building is flanked by shops. The arch, above which are 2 storeys of offices, leads through to a courtyard and the unimposing 3-storey premises of Dickens Bros., leather factors, one of only two such companies still operating in the county.

271 Former GM Tebbutt shoe factory
SP 762612 ★
The 3-storey factory on the corner of Clare St/Grove Rd was built in 1889 for GM Tebbutt and operational until 1968. The frontage on Clare St has 4 gable ends with diaper brickwork, that on Grove Rd has two gable ends, the one further from Clare St being of later design. Now converted to apartments under the name *Grove Works*.

272 Former Allinson shoe factory
SP 759612 ★
At the corner of Clare St and Earl St is the relatively plain 3-storey plus basement factory of Allinson. A window sill at the corner carries the date 1888.

273 Former leather factory, Gray St
SP 760613 ★ LBII
On the north side of Gray St at No. 3. Three storeys plus semi-basement factory with 5-bay frontage containing taking-in door in centre of top floor with Dutch gable above and wall mounted crane to one side. Range of 3-storey buildings to the rear forming an 'F' shape, the interior containing cast-iron pillars. Built c1892 by Mr Dyer a currier but used by a variety of leather and shoe companies as well as other trades over the years. Now converted to apartments.

274 Former shoe factories in Shakespeare Rd
SP 761613 ★
In Shakespeare Rd are several former 3 or 4 storey shoe factories with relatively little embellishment, mostly converted to apartments with plastic windows. They are at the junctions with Hervey St, Cowper St, Hood St and Burns St.

275 Former shoemakers' workshops
SP 761615 ★ LBII
Nos. 41 and 43 Colwyn Rd are brick-built terraced houses with two storeys plus attic constructed c1885. Behind these are large workshops occupied in the late 19thC and early 20thC by boot closers or closed upper makers.

276 Former racecourse pavilion
SP 764616 ★ LBII

On the west side of Kettering Rd, ¾ mile north-east of the town centre. Racing offic-ially started on the Freemen's Commons next to Kettering Rd in 1727 and continued until 1904 when an increasing number of accidents caused the Jockey Club to declare the course unfit for racing. The former grandstand dates from the first half of the 19thC and is now in use as a sports pavilion (ground floor) and restaurant (1st floor). It is a large stuccoed building and somewhat difficult to envisage as a grandstand now that the raked seating has long been removed from its roof.

277 JL & Co. shoe factory
SP 765621 ★ LBII

On the south side of Oliver St near its junct-ion with Kettering Rd, 1 mile north-east of the town centre. Three-storey shoe factory built c1895 in a T plan, with a wall-mounted crane at the rear. Used by Singlehurst & Gulliver till the mid 1920s, then by Edward Green. Now used by JL & Co. to produce men's high quality footwear. The interior retains many original fixtures and fittings.

NORTHAMPTON – NORTH-EAST

278 Streetscape of former shoe factories and housing between Kettering Rd and Wellingborough Rd

A variety of mainly 3-storey shoe factories built from the late 1880s interspersed among terraced housing, ½ mile north-east of the town centre. Key sites are detailed below (sites 279-284).

279 Former Manfield shoe factory
SP 772613 ★ LBII

On the north side of Wellingborough Rd, one mile east of the town centre. The firm of Manfield and Sons was founded in 1819, occupying an early factory in Campbell Square from 1857 (demolished in 1984). The Welling-borough Rd factory, constructed in 1892, was the first to be built on a single floor and covered four acres. The frontage included a two-storey office block. It is of red brick with stone window frames and stone banding. Later part of the British Shoe Corporation, the factory finally closed in 1992 and only the office block facing onto Wellingborough Rd remains.

280 Crockett & Jones shoe factory
SP 766614 ★ LBII

Facing onto Perry St, Magee St and Turner St. This extensive range of 2, 3 and 4-storey buildings was built from 1889 onwards for Crockett & Jones. The two-storey block facing onto Magee St has a stone pediment and cornices. Behind are two-storey blocks with roof lights. On Turner St is a 4-storey steel-framed block with large windows, built in 1910 and possibly the first steel framed building in Northampton. Crockett & Jones was founded in 1879 and still manufactures men's high quality welted footwear on this site.

276 Former racecourse pavilion, Kettering Rd, Northampton

281 Former shoe factories in Henry St
SP 764613 ★
On the south side of Henry St is a range of 3-storey factories. The most easterly one, No. 52, dating from 1890 with twin triangular pediments was the premises of J Branch. No. 50 with the single pediment was firstly the premises of Eyre Bros., later Arnold Bros. (see Site 282).

282 Former Normal Boot & Shoe Factory
SP 764612 ★
On the north side of Talbot Rd is a 3-storey factory with the date 1889 and *Normal Boot & Shoe Factory* in stone on a triangular pediment. It was built for Stubbs & Grimsdell, later becoming E Grimsdell. It is claimed to be the first shoe factory in the town where all production operations were undertaken 'in-house'. In about 1909 it was taken over by Arnold Bros. who used the factory along with premises at 50 Henry St (see Site 281) until at least the 1960s. Now converted to apartments.

283 Former shoe factory in Artizan Rd
SP 766612 ★
In Artizan Rd at its junction with Billington St is a 3-storey factory with pedimented corner porch dating from the 1880s. It was at one time used by James Branch and later Crockett & Jones before their move to Perry St.

284 Former Sears shoe factory
SP 768614 ★
The extensive Sears *Truefom* shoe factory stood on the corner of Stimpson Ave and Adnitt Rd. Today only the highly decorated 3-storey office block in Adnitt Rd remains, built in 1913 and now called *Sears House.*

NORTHAMPTON – EAST

285 Streetscape of former shoe factories and housing between Wellingborough Rd and Billing Rd
In this area ½ mile east of the town centre, are a number of former shoe factories dating from the 1870s interspersed among terraced housing. All are now in other uses. Key sites are detailed below (sites 286-288).

286 Former shoe factory, Palmerston Rd
SP 764608 ★
On the west side of Palmerston Rd is an attractive 7 bay, 3-storey shoe factory with ornamented brickwork, round-headed upper windows and wall-mounted crane. Used by a variety of companies over the years and now converted to apartments.

287 Former shoe factory, Ethel St
SP 764607 ★
On the corner of Ethel St and Woodford St is a large factory, 3-storeys plus basement, in red brick with curved stone window lintels extended to provide a pronounced stone string course. There is a datestone for 1875 and a wall-mounted crane is adjacent to the doors at the 2nd floor level. Between the two world wars it was occupied by Haynes & Cann. Now converted to apartments called *The Works.*

288 Former shoe factory, Palmerston Rd / Stockley St
SP 765607 ★
On the south-east corner of Palmerston Rd and Stockley St, *Hamilton House* is a three-storey brick building of three bays on each of the sides facing a road. Each bay on the ground floor has a large semi-circular window surmounted by a prominent stone arch. Above and below the second-storey windows on both frontages are stone string courses. It was used as a shoe factory from c1890, firstly by J&J Brown, later by A Jones and in the 1950s by Church's Shoes.

282 Facade of former Normal Boot & Shoe Factory, Talbot Rd, Northampton

286 Former shoe factory, Palmerston Rd, Northampton

289 Former CWS shoe factory
SP 773612 ★ LBII
On the south side of Christchurch Rd, one mile east of the town centre. A two-storey dark-red brick office building is the remains of the former CWS shoe factory built in 1924. The façade is of classical design, with a Venetian window at first floor level below the pediment. In 1969 it was acquired by Mobbs Miller, last manufacturers and suppliers to the shoe industry but is now offices, albeit under the name *Mobbs House*.

290 Former Co-op bakery
SP 770610 ★
On the west of Barry Rd, at its junction with Wellingborough Rd, ¾ mile east of the town centre. The Northampton Co-operative Society Ltd.'s bakery of 1912 was originally of 3-storeys plus an attic storey. Three of the bays are carried up to dormer windows. Mainly of red brick, the windows have stone lintels and sills, and the brick pilasters, where they change in thickness above the first-storey have stone consoles placed vertically. The ground floor has lost its windows in the conversion to a supermarket.

291 Abington Park water tower
SP 777618 ★ LBII C
In the eastern part of Abington Park, one mile east of the town centre, situated between Wellingborough Rd and the top lake. The square stone tower has a pyramidal slate roof and two buttresses on the southern side. Built in 1678 to supply water to Abington Manor, it was referred to in a sale notice of 1840 and still houses the remains of a wooden water-wheel which powered a reciprocating pump. There is a dovecote under the roof.

292 Abington Park bandstand
SP 773615 ★ C
In the west part of Abington Park. Erected when the park was opened in 1897. An elegant structure with cast-iron columns supporting a leaded, reverse-arched roof.

293 Abington Museum
SP 775615 ○ LBI C
In the 15thC manor house on the west side of Park Avenue South. It Includes the Museum of Leathercraft. Although the displays focus on social history, costume and military history, the temporary exhibitions often involve the town's industrial heritage. Free admission Apr-Oct, Thu-Sun (www.northampton.gov.uk).

NORTHAMPTON – SOUTH-EAST

294 Former electricity generating station
SP 762598 ★
Situated on the east side of Nunn Mills Rd immediately south of the River Nene, ¾ mile south-east of the town centre. Using steam turbines to generate alternating current, this power station came on load in 1919 and soon became known as Hardingstone Junction power station. It was built by the Northampton Electric Light & Power Company (NELPCo) to augment its first power station in Angel Lane, where supply of electricity commenced in 1891. This large brick building is now roofless and without a back wall.

295 Chimney for former sewage pumping station
SP 767599 ★
South of Bedford Rd, almost opposite the junction with Cliftonville Rd, 1 mile south-east

of the town centre, stands an ornate stone chimney. This is the only survival from the engine house built to accommodate a 12 horsepower steam engine in 1862 to improve the town's sewage disposal arrangements. The sewage treatment works on this site closed after land filtration areas, for treatment of the town's sewage by broad irrigation, were laid out at Billing in 1875.

295 Chimney for former sewage pumping station, Bedford Rd, Northampton

296 Former Midland Railway locoshed
SP 761596 ☐ LBII
Behind Avon Cosmetics and some 100yds west of the footpath which extends south of Nunn Mills Rd, approximately ¾ mile south-east of the town centre. The former Midland Railway locomotive shed was built in 1873 to serve the line from Northampton (St. Johns) to Bedford. Constructed of red brick, it has blind arches on the side walls lined in white bricks. More recently used as a welding school for British Rail Engineering, it is now disused and has been partly damaged by fire. The site is currently inaccessible, being surrounded by Railtrack's steel fencing.

297 River navigation channel
SP 758599 ★
About 400yds east of South Bridge, ½ mile south-east of the town centre, the River Nene divides into two. Its original course is the southern channel leading towards the site of Nunn Mills. The other channel was constructed to make the river navigable from the sea as far as Northampton. This was opened in 1761. The artificial cut rejoins the old course of the river a short distance east of Nunn Mills Rd.

NORTHAMPTON – SOUTH-CENTRAL

298 Beckett's Well
SP 760602 ★ LBII
Situated on the north side of Bedford Rd, just east of its junction with Victoria Promenade. The so-called *Thomas-à-Beckett Well* is on the site of a 13thC well. The open-fronted stone building with a pitched slate roof is the result of rebuilding in 1845 by Edward Harrison Barwell celebrating his final year as Mayor. He was an ironfounder in the town and one of the bollards at the entrance to the well carries the name of the firm.

299 Former cattle market buildings
SP 756601 ★
On the south side of Victoria Promenade in a supermarket car park. Matching gatehouses, either side of the former main entrance, are all that now remains of Northampton's live-stock market. These survivors are two-storey red brick with limestone string courses and steep, slated roofs. Each has a single-storey extension to the rear, one of which had a clock in its gable that could be seen from most parts of the market. The cattle market opened in 1873 on this purpose-built site and apart from the gatehouses was demolished in 1997.

300 Former gas company offices
SP 751601 ★
On the east side of the junction of St. Peter's Way and Towcester Rd. The substantial two-storey red brick building with a hipped slate

roof has decorative brickwork at first floor level and at the eaves. It is of seven bays with a central doorway, over which, in brick, is the name *Northampton Gas Light Company*. It was erected in 1880 and was the main office of the company until 1908 when a new showroom and central office was brought into use in Abington St.

301 Gas holders
SP 750602 & SP 750600 ★

On either side of Towcester Rd near its junction with St. Peter's Way stand two 19thC gas holders erected by the former Northampton Gas Light Company. Both are under threat of demolition.

302 Former Latimer & Crick warehouse
SP 755598 ★

On the north bank of the River Nene, immediately east of South Bridge. A large four-storey, brick-built 19thC warehouse used for storing grain, having wooden lucams at both the river and opposite ends of the building. Formerly used by Latimer and Crick, agricultural suppliers but now converted to apartments.

NORTHAMPTON – FAR-COTTON

303 Former Midland Railway granary
SP 755596 ★ **LBII**

In Cotton End, 100yds north of the former Bridge St level crossing. A three-storey ware-

house constructed c1880 by the Midland Railway for storing grain. It is mainly of brick although part of the south wall is of stone where it once abutted an adjacent building. It has been recently restored and converted to offices with the name *Old Granary*.

304 Former railway houses
SP 756595 ★

In Claughton Rd, off Ransome Rd east of Cotton End. A small estate of houses was built in 1915 by the LNWR, in connection with its new sleeper and permanent way depot, which was located alongside the Northampton to Peterborough line in Far Cotton. A total of nineteen houses were built, consisting of eight pairs of semi-detached workmen's houses, one pair of larger semi-detached managers' houses, and a single detached property for the yard master. The road was named after Sir Gilbert Claughton, the then Chairman of the company. The houses are still in largely original condition although with modern updating of details.

305 Former LNWR locoshed
SP 753595 ★

Some 200yds west of the former Bridge St level crossing, best viewed from Pomfret Arms Close, off Old Towcester Rd. A locoshed has been on this site since 1847 and the present brick building with clerestory roof replaced the original in 1855 with an extension to the west in 1871. When a new locoshed was

305 Former LNWR locoshed, Far Cotton, Northampton

309 Former maltings, St. James Rd, Northampton

constructed further west in 1881 it became a carriage shed and was later used for track engineering purposes.

306 Former van builder's premises
SP 754597 ★

On the west side of Cotton End a little south of South Bridge. Premises formerly used to build and repair horse-drawn vans. Facing Cotton End, Nos. 2 & 4 are three-storey stone buildings. No.2 has large double doors on the ground floor. By 1899 the room behind was used as a coach showroom. Alterations in the southern approach to South Bridge have left a step down from the present road level on to the floor of the showroom. In and around the yard to the west are buildings associated with the van business at the end of the 19thC. On the north side, the single-storey buildings were the body shop, wheelwrights' shop and smith (nearest the entrance to the yard). A raising and lowering tyring platform over a pit survives near the west boundary as does the brick tyring furnace. Other buildings are associated with the present-day business of JE Matthews and Sons Ltd. blacksmiths and welders.

307 Canal lock
SP 753597 ★

Reached from Old Towcester Rd which heads west from Cotton End. Lock No.17 is the termination of the Northampton branch canal opened by the Grand Junction Canal Comp-

any in 1815. The lock provides connection with the River Nene navigation. Immediately west of the lock, an angle to the south in the canal bank indicates the original course of the canal before it was diverted in 1879 to allow development of the railway yards and locomotive depot to the south.

NORTHAMPTON – HUNSBURY

308 Hunsbury Hill Ironstone Railway Museum
SP 734585 ○

Access from Hunsbury Hill Rd opposite St. Benedicts Church, 1½ miles south-west of the town centre. The base of Northamptonshire Ironstone Railway Trust since 1975, it is on the site of part of the former quarries which served Hunsbury Hill Furnaces. The museum has a variety of industrial locomotives and rolling stock. Rides are provided on a loop of standard gauge track. There are also a series of models showing different aspects of iron ore extraction. (www.nirt.co.uk)

NORTHAMPTON – ST. JAMES

309 Former maltings
SP 746603 ★

South of St. James Rd just west of its bridge over the railway. The maltings were built in 1888 for Thomas Manning & Co. of the Castle Brewery which stood on the other side of the river, east of the railway. It is a brick building of three storeys with eleven bays, except at the east end which housed the two kilns, with distinctive steeply pitched pyramidal roofs. The malting is reputed to have been the first in the country to have a concrete floor. After the brewery had become a subsidiary of P Phipps & Co. Ltd., the building was used as a bonded warehouse but since 1994 part of it has been used for the Frog Island Brewery.

310 Church's Shoes St. James factory
SP 743605 ★

On the south-west side of St. James Rd, ¼ mile west of the railway station. The extensive shoe factory premises were originally occupied from 1905 by Padmore and Barnes. Their motif, a Native American, is still present in the form of a wall plaque. In 1957 Church's Shoes, who still manufacture mens' high quality welted footwear, moved here from their Duke St factory (see Site 263). The main office building fronting onto St. James Rd has a clerestory style roof.

311 Bus garage and former tram depot
SP 742605 ★

On the south-west side of St. James Rd, approximately ½ mile west of the railway station. The original red brick car sheds of Northampton Corporation Tramways consisted of two clerestory roofed bays with circular vents in the upper gables each with three semi-circular arched entrances for the tramcars. The contractor in 1904 was Watkin Bros. and the cost to the Corporation for the initial construction was £4,057.12s.5d. With the later acquisition of fresh batches of cars, extensions to the sheds were erected to the east and west of the original building and once buses took over, from 1934 onwards, a very large western extension was erected. The architecture of each fresh extension showed progressively less adornment. Tram rails remain in the floor in the easternmost shed.

312 National Lift Tower
SP 734605 ★ LBII

South of Weedon Rd about ¾ mile west of the railway station. Formerly known as the

Express Lift Tower; this 418ft (127m) high lift-testing tower was built in 1982 using an innovative continuous concrete casting process. The architects were Stimpson & Walton of Northampton and the builders Tileman & Co. of London. The tower was part of the Abbey Works, established by Smith, Major and Stevens Ltd. in 1909, later merged with the Express Lift Company and subsequently acquired by the General Electric Company. After the company was taken over by OTIS in 1996, the works were closed in 1999 and, except for the tower, demolished and the site developed for housing. After an uncertain period in which an application to demolish the tower was refused, the tower is now privately owned and is once again used as a research, development and lift testing facility.

NORTON   A2
313 Norton canal junction
SP 602657 ★ C

Reached by taking the canal tow-path west from the A5, some 4 miles north-west of its junction with the A45 at Weedon. The Grand Junction Canal was joined here in 1814 by the Grand Union Canal, which connected with the Leicester and Northampton Union Canal at Foxton. The former toll-house in the west corner of the junction, was built in 1914, when the gauging point for boats was moved here from lock No.9. Today it is a holiday cottage.

313 Canal milepost, Norton Junction

Boats were gauged under bridge No.10 (LBII), to calculate tolls to be paid. This bridge was built with ramps for horses to cross the former Grand Junction Canal but they had to cross the Leicester Arm by a swing bridge, which after being hit by a pleasure boat has now been replaced by a stepped footbridge built on its abutments. In the grass on the toll-house side is a metal rail on an arc of brickwork, part of the turntable on which the old bridge pivoted. Note also the GJCCo milepost (LBII) located on the side of the tow-path at the start of the Leicester line.

314 Canal lock
SP 606656 ★ C

Alongside the A5 road bridge is the top lock (No.7) of the Whilton and Buckby flight of wide locks, built in 1796. It has a 9ft (2.7m) fall. When water was in short supply, the water level in the summit pound was so low that fully laden boats could not pass out of this lock and all canal traffic stopped. The capacity of the summit pound was increased by raising the banks by a foot, and adding four extra courses of bricks to the walls of this and Braunston top lock at the other end of the summit. A side-pond built to the east of this lock to save water has been filled in. For the other locks in the flight see under Long Buckby and Whilton.

OLD   B3

315 Former brewery
SP 788734 ★

Situated behind the house now known as *Brewery Farm* (LBII), at the junction of Mill Lane and the road to Broughton. The long two-storey brick building at right angles to the Faxton road was part of the brewery operated by the Tomblin family from c1854 till 1906.

OUNDLE   D4

Unusually in Northamptonshire, this market town never saw the industrial developments based on textiles, footwear and engineering which were common elsewhere. Brewing was the most significant industry well into the 20thC and several sites remain.

316 Oundle Museum
TL 036880 ○ C

In *The Courthouse*, on the west side of Mill Rd, a short distance north of the junction with South Rd, the museum has displays on the town's brewing industry and local crafts. (www.oundlemuseum.org.uk)

317 Former Anchor Brewery & maltings
TL 037879 ★ C

In the south-east corner of the junction of South Rd with Mill Rd. The former Anchor Brewery was founded in 1854. The brewery was in the three-storey brick building with a hipped slate roof, whose length is along South Rd. At the west end is a substantial brewer's house of two storeys. A large arch at the east end of the brewery building leads into a long yard with, on the east side, a two-storey stone malthouse with a pyramidal-roofed kiln at the south end. Brewing ceased in 1906 after which the premises were used by a boot and shoe factor. They are now occupied as a private dwelling and studios.

318 Former Union Brewery maltings
TL 038880 ★ C

Extending northwards from South Rd, east of Danford Close, are the former maltings for Oundle Union Brewery. This long two-storey stone building has been converted to dwellings.

318 Former Union Brewery maltings, Oundle

319 Former Union Brewery
TL 039880 ★ C

Situated between West St and South Rd, the Oundle Union Brewery was established in

1836 by six local farmers and businessmen. In a builders merchant's yard accessed between 36 and 42 West St, the yellow brick brewhouse is of five bays parallel to South Rd and of four bays along the alley which runs past the east end. The brewery offices were at the West St entrance to the brewery, in premises now known as *Townley House*. Brewing ceased in 1853 after the business was purchased by Smith & Co., then the largest brewers in Oundle.

320 Sign from former brewery
TL 041881 ★ C
In the yard behind the *Talbot Hotel* in New St, in the upper storey of the range of buildings (LBI) on the south side. A rather weatherworn carved stone tablet carries the initials *JS* above three casks under which is the date *1775*. This commemorates the beginning of brewing by John Smith, the founder of Smith and Co., Oundle. It had been on the east side of Smith's brewery at the end of North St until 1963 when brewing ceased.

321 Former Smith & Co. maltings
TL 043885 ★ LBII C
Situated in the angle between North St and East Rd, the former Smith & Co.'s No.2 maltings is a two-storey stone building, with a lucam on the North St side. The kiln was at the end embraced by the corner of East Rd. Malting ceased in 1947 and the premises have been converted to apartments under the name *Fotheringhay Mews*.

322 Former Oundle station
TL 047890 ★ LBII
North-west of the roundabout where the roads to Oundle and Ashton join the A605. Opened in 1845 on the LNWR's Northampton to Peterborough line, the station buildings are of stone with numerous gables and tall chimneys. Regular passenger services ceased in 1964 but the station continued in regular use until the 1980s by special trains for Oundle School pupils at the beginning and end of term, after which the track was removed. The platforms remain but the buildings have been converted to a dwelling.

322 Former Oundle station

323 Former river wharf
TL 043888 ★
The site of Oundle Wharf is adjacent to Station Rd where it crosses the River Nene about 400yds before it reaches the A605. Most of the wharf buildings have been demolished or converted to dwellings (some LBII).

324 Former railway viaduct incorporated into road bridge
TL 048870 ★
A modern road bridge carries the A605 Oundle bypass over the River Nene, southeast of the town. It incorporates the original blue-brick arched railway viaduct built to carry the LNWR's Northampton to Peterborough line, which closed in 1966. The original arches are on the west side having been extended in width with matching blue brick to accommodate the road. Best viewed from the river.

PASSENHAM   B1
325 Former watermill
SP 782393 ★
On the River Great Ouse, west of the road between the roundabout on the A422 near Deanshanger, and Calverton. The corn mill is a two-storey stone building with a red tiled roof. The central bay has a triangular pediment, possibly indicating the position of the lucam, with segmental-arched windows on the ground floor and an older rectangular window at the south end of the upper storey. Before milling ceased c1920, two wooden waterwheels of 12ft (3.6m) diameter were in use. Now converted to a dwelling, apparently by

blocking up most of the upper-storey windows and inserting dormers at the eaves and windows in the roof.

PAULERSPURY B1
326 Water stand-pipe
SP 716454 ★
In Park Lane, opposite its junction with Lumber Lane. A cast-iron stand-pipe about 3ft (1m) high, having a fluted column topped by a dome with a knob on top, still working. It carries the maker's name *BLAKEBOROUGH* on its base.

327 Sir Henry Royce Memorial Foundation
SP 720455 ❑
Housed in *Hunt House* (LBII), High St, Paulerspury, almost opposite the turn into Lumber Lane, this is a comprehensive collection of documents and photographs illustrating the history of Rolls Royce and Sir Henry Royce, the car's creator. (www.henryroyce.org.uk)

PITSFORD B2
328 Northampton & Lamport Railway
SP 735667 ○
About ½ mile east of Chapel Brampton on the road to Pitsford. A heritage steam railway is based at the site of *Pitsford & Brampton* station on the former LNWR's Northampton to Market Harborough line. None of the original buildings remain. The railway operates approximately 1½ miles of track and has a number of working steam and diesel locos as well as a variety of rolling stock. Trains operate at weekends and bank holidays between March and November (www.nlr.org.uk). Just beyond the southern limit of the relaid track, the former crossing keeper's cottage remains, much altered and extended, adjacent to where the trackbed crossed the A5199.

POTTERSPURY B1
329 Former watermill
SP 761433 ★ LBII
On the Potterspury Brook, a tributary of the River Great Ouse and best viewed from Potterspury churchyard. A three-storey stone

326 Water stand-pipe, Paulerspury

corn mill with a central projection on the upstream side. It has round-headed windows with brick arches, and the slate roof continues across the adjoining mill cottage of only two storeys. By the 1860s a steam engine had been installed and with the water-wheel was driving four pairs of stones through bevel gears from a layshaft. Flour milling ceased around 1950. In 1954 the mill pond was filled in although gristing continued, using a drive from a tractor until about 1960 after which most of the machinery was stripped out. Converted to dwellings, although the tall brick chimney still stands.

RAUNDS D3
330 Remains of brickworks
TL 003725 ★
Adjacent to a track leading from Mountbatten Way to the former Manor Farm, on the eastern side of the town. Manor Brickworks operated on this site between 1898 and 1974 and was the last one to operate in the county. There is little that is identifiable except for the remains of a limekiln and a circular wash pit. The limekiln (LBII) was unusual, a circular brick-built structure which had a conical top, now fallen in. At one time it was converted for firing experimental bricks. The wash pit was used to separate out lumps of gypsum

from the clay. It consists of a circular brick trough in which a series of ploughs and harrows would have revolved around a central vertical shaft.

331 Gateway into former Wellington tannery
SP 993722 ★
On the north side of Wellington Rd, 100yds east of its junction with London Rd and Chelveston Rd. A stone and brick arch between two rows of terraced houses carries the name *Wellington Works*, surmounted by a Wellington boot. It was the entrance to the former Wellington tannery, converted from a shoe factory in WW1 and is now all that remains.

332 Former Chambers heel factory
TL 001729 ★ LBII
In Park Rd opposite its junction with Manor St. The two-storey building in white Whittlesey brick was formerly Ernest Chambers' factory for the manufacture of shoe heels. Gold-painted ball finials mounted at each end of the parapet apparently came from the tithe barn and it is purported that a Wellington boot once adorned the centre pediment. The factory was subsequently used by Wescom Engineering but is currently empty.

333 Former waterworks
SP 978728 ★
Close by the A45 at the end of Meadow Lane, a track which leads west from London Rd opposite Marshalls Rd. A group of single-storey brick buildings, previously in a ruinous state but recently partly refurbished. A date of 1908 is in the stone curved pediment over the entrance facing on to the track. The main well, 18ft (5.5m) deep and 16ft (4.9m) diameter was near the pumping station. This housed a 30 horsepower crude oil engine working a diaphragm pump to lift the water to a covered reservoir on the road to Hargrave, from which it ran by gravity into the town.

334 Former Raunds station
TL 020737 ★
Adjacent to the B663, 1½ miles east of the town. The former station and goods yard opened in 1866 on the Midland Railway's Kettering to Huntingdon line. The station closed to passengers in 1959 and the building has been converted to a dwelling. The yard is used by an auto repair & salvage company.

RAVENSTHORPE   B3
335 Ravensthorpe reservoir & former waterworks
SP 681702 ★
The entrance to the public car park is on the north-west side of the road from Teeton to Ravensthorpe. The reservoir was constructed

332 Former Chambers heel factory, Park Rd, Raunds

by Northampton Corporation to supply water to the town. Work started in 1886 and the first water was pumped to the town in 1890. When full, the reservoir holds 40 million gallons of water. Below the dam are the single-storey buildings of the pumping station. The building nearest to the dam was the coal store, the next was for the boilers and buildings at right angles to these held steam engines and pumps, all of which have been replaced by electric pumps. Between the buildings and the road are the sand filter beds. Parts of the railway which moved the sand for cleaning are now at the Irchester Narrow Gauge Railway Museum (see Site 157).

RINGSTEAD D3

336 Former Ringstead Britannia Co-op Society shoe factory
SP 989752 ★
On the east side of Denford Rd at its junction with Gladstone St. The three-storey shoe factory in white brick with decorated red-brick banding was built by the Ringstead Britannia Co-operative Society Limited. It is now converted to offices but a circular motif remains on the front wall.

337 Former stone railway sleeper blocks
SP 967745 ★
On a footpath from the Addingtons to Ringstead, adjacent to Upper Ringstead Lock on the River Nene and close to the site of *Ringstead & Addington* station on the former LNWR's Northampton to Peterborough line. Former London & Birmingham Railway stone sleeper blocks were used as stepping stones along the footpath in this low-lying area, although they are now covered in undergrowth in summer. Reputedly transported along the LNWR when the L&B track was re-laid. Surprisingly not all the same type of stone.

337 Former railway stone sleeper block used as stepping stone, Ringstead

ROADE B2

338 Roade cutting
SP 755516 to 746532 ★
Can be viewed from the bridge carrying the A508 over the West Coast Main Line at Roade; also from the Courteenhall to Blis-

worth road. The 1½ mile long, 60ft (20m) deep cutting was dug through limestone on clay to carry the London & Birmingham Railway between Denbigh Hall and Rugby in 1838. It was deepened and widened in 1875 to take the extra tracks for the Northampton loop. The latter had to be strengthened with 'grid-iron' girders after a landslip in 1891. At SP 752521 an aqueduct (LBII), dating from c1838 and consisting of a cast-iron channel supported on sandstone piers, carries a small stream over the cutting.

ROTHERSTHORPE B2

339 Flight of canal locks
SP 723560 - 724581 ★ LBII
Most of this flight of 13 narrow locks within a mile, on the Northampton branch of the Grand Union Canal, can be seen from Bridge No.4, the Rothersthorpe to Milton Malsor road crossing. On the east side of the top lock is a former lock house, two-storeys, with a low pitched hipped roof and wide eaves, dating from 1815 but modernised in 1988. Below the fifth lock is a wooden lifting bridge with massive overhead balance beams. A similar bridge is further down the flight. The extra wide area on the tow-path side is purported to have accommodated the 1805 - 1815 tramroad to Northampton.

ROTHWELL C3

340 Market hall
SP 817812 ★ LBI C
On Market Hill a two-storey, oblong, limestone-built structure with four oblong projections giving it a cruciform plan. It was erected in the 1570s by Sir Thomas Tresham whose family seat was at nearby Rushton Hall. The family's trade-mark trefoil embellishments adorn the market house. The ground floor was originally open, for market use, and the building remained incomplete for more than 300 years until it was roofed in 1895.

341 Heritage Centre
SP 816812 ◯ C
On the north side of Bridge St at Nos.14-16. Rothwell Heritage Centre contains exhibits

and artefacts relating to local industries and including the boot & shoe trade. (www.rothwellheritage.org.uk)

342 Former fire station
SP 815813 ★

On the north side of the bend in School Lane and situated between Ashgate Court and Leys Ave. The fire station was built in 1909. The gable end facing south formerly had large double doors but these have been replaced by large windows. Now used as offices.

343 Former Crispin Shoe Works
SP 817811 ★ C

To the left of and behind 1-4 Well Lane (LBII), at the south end of Market Hill. The front two-storey factory dates from 1902 and is of similar style to the adjacent owner's house. Behind is a range of brick and stone buildings, which dates from the late 18thC. The factory, now converted into apartments, was operated by S Sarjeant & Co. until at least the 1960s.

344 Remains of ironstone quarry
SP 817822 ★

Immediately north of Grange Farm, the remains of ironstone quarrying can be clearly seen extending west from Shotwell Mill Lane off Rushton Rd. These workings, dating from the 1920s were at the eastern end of Rothwell Hill Quarries owned by Stanton Ironworks Co. The National Strike of 1926 resulted in the closure of the workings, leaving a section of the exposed ironstone bed intact.

345 Former shoe outworkers' workshops
SP 818814 ★

Between New St and Tresham St is a row of single-storey garden workshops known locally as 'barns'. These were built for use by shoe outworkers in the late 19thC. Similar single and 2-storey workshops also exist behind terraced houses in other parts of the town.

RUSHDEN C2

From about 1880 the footwear industry in Rushden expanded at a remarkable rate. The

consequent growth in population led to a range of public facilities being established within a 20 year period. These included a piped water supply from a new reservoir at Sywell, some 10 miles distant – see Site 384, an electricity generating plant and an expanded gas works. By the 1930s, the Midland Railway branch line (with outsize goods shed to cater for the bulky footwear traffic) was sadly found wanting and an enterprising London-based coach company provided an alternative service with an ultra-modern 1930s building to match.

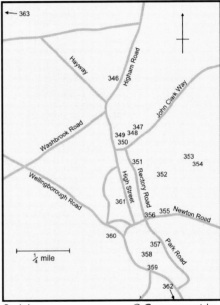

Rushden   © Crown copyright

346 Former John White shoe factory
SP 956676 ★ LBII

At the junction of Lime St and Higham Rd, ½ mile north of the town centre. This art-deco style shoe factory was built for footwear company John White Footwear Ltd. in 1938. It was designed by Professor (Sir Albert) Richardson, and has a frontage of white-painted brick and glass with a protruding *piano nobile* reached by an outside staircase. The whole building is contained in a large area of garden. The factory closed in the 1990s and has been converted to apartments.

349 Former Birch Bros. coach station, Higham Rd, Rushden

349 Former Birch Bros. coach station
SP 957673 ★

In Higham Rd just north of the town centre. The mid-1930s saw a futuristic addition to the Rushden skyline with the construction of Birch Bros. coach station. A conventional north-light, saw-tooth roofed garage (visible from Shirley Road) was fronted by a stuccoed art-deco block consisting of an off-centre entrance for vehicles and pedestrians, flanked on the north side by a three-storey block with flat roof, curved corners and metal windows. The top storey is continued over the main entrance and joins a striking tower, semicircular fronted in plan with a central pilaster continuing up over the curved-top roof. Now used partly as a furniture showroom, partly as a food takeaway.

347 Former John White transport depot
SP 958673 ★

On the south side of Shirley Rd, to the north of the town centre. A single-storey brick garage building constructed in the 1920s. In the gable end above the sliding doors on the front elevation is: *Transport Depot of John White (Impregnable Boots) Ltd.* (See also Sites 153 & 346)

348 Former electricity works
SP 958673 ★

On the south side of Shirley Rd is the former generating station of the Rushden and District Electric Supply Co. Ltd. which began its public supply on 15 October 1913 with two 240 horsepower diesel generating sets. The large brick building presents a gable end on to the road. It had two very large windows with semi-circular tops, now bricked in, and large double doors, also with semi-circular top. By 1924 generating had ceased after the company had been acquired by the Northampton Electric Light & Power Co. Ltd. who supplied the area from its Hardingstone Junction station.

350 Preserved Rushden station and former goods shed
SP 957672 ○ C

On John Clark Way, the new link road connecting Rushden with the A6 by-pass, opposite its junction with Rectory Road. The station, constructed of brick, was opened in 1894 on the Midland Railway's Higham Ferrers branch. Closed in 1959, the site was later taken over by the Rushden Historical Transport Society (www.rhts.co.uk) as their headquarters and is now the home of Rushden Transport Museum. The preserved station buildings house a wide range of mainly transport-related artefacts. Steam & diesel hauled services operate on a length of track which extends towards Higham Ferrers on most summer weekends. The former goods shed survives as a council depot but is now separated from the station by the aforementioned link road.

351 Former DenBros shoe factory
SP 958670 ★

On Rectory Rd near its junction with Albert Rd, immediately to the north-east of the town centre. This former shoe factory was built c1890 for E Claridge & Sons. It was taken over in the 1930s by Denton Brothers (DB Shoes) and used by them until c1980. It is single storey with a two-storey red brick office block fronting onto Rectory Rd. Notable for its shaped gable with stone cornice and diaper brickwork patterns of varying size.

352 Former Fred Hawkes shoe machinery works
SP 960669 ★

On the north side of Portland Rd, immediately to the east of the town centre. This unimposing single-storey building with red and blue brick frontage was built in the late 1920s. It was formerly the shoe machinery works of Fred Hawkes and is notable for its painted foyer which depicted the company's activities.

353 Grenson shoe factory, Queen St, Rushden

353 Grenson shoe factory
SP 962671 ★ LBII

At the junction of Queen St and Cromwell Rd, ¼ mile north-east of the town centre. A four-storey brick-built factory constructed in 1895 for William Green (Grenson) when they moved from their original factory on High St

South (Site 359). The factory has been extended several times and still produces men's welted footwear. It has iron-framed windows with segmental arches on the lower floors and twin rectangular windows on the top floor. It is notable for the octagonal corner turret with small pedimented, louvred dormer windows in alternate faces.

354 Former Rushden Steam Laundry
SP 962670 ★

On the south side of Allen Rd between Cromwell Rd and Lawton Rd, ¼ mile north-east of the town centre. A single-storey red brick building, constructed in 1895 as Rushden Steam Laundry. It was converted for use as a heel factory between 1906 and 1922 and occupied by P Collins until at least 1967. A brass plate on the door indicates that it was later used by HW Chapman, cardboard box manufacturer, presumably as an extension of their factory opposite.

355 Former fire station
SP 960667 ★

On the north side of Newton Rd just west of Robinson Rd. Built in 1902, the former engine house is a two-storey red brick building with stone window surrounds and dentillation at the eaves. The large double-doors have been removed and the ground floor frontage much altered. Adjacent to the engine house on its west side is the former station house, two storeys with a bay on the ground floor. Behind is a brick hose-drying tower with louvred oval windows in the upper storey and surmounted by a red-tiled splay-footed pyramidal roof.

356 Former bus garage
SP 959666 ★

At the junction of Newton Rd and Rectory Rd in the town centre. This building represents perhaps the best of United Counties Omnibus Co.'s attempts to improve the streetscapes of the towns in which they operated. Its pleasing lines, not quite so visible since its closure as a bus garage c1978, date from 1938 when H&J Taylor (Contractors) Ltd. of London erected it.

357 Former Cunnington Bros. shoe factory
SP 960664 ★ LBII C

On Park Rd at its junction with Crabb St, ¼ mile to the south-east of the town centre. The façade of this 3-storey shoe factory has Flemish-bond bricks, the red stretchers and white headers creating a chequer pattern. There are loading doors on the Park Rd frontage and two windows surmounted by triangular pediments to the side elevation. Built for Cunnington Bros. in the 1880s and extended in the 1890s, it was later used by Bignells. Currently empty awaiting redevelopment.

358 Former Walter Sargent shoe factory
SP 959664 ★ LBII C

On the north side of Crabb St (No.7), ¼ mile to the south-east of the town centre. A large 3-storey plus basement shoe factory with cast-iron wall mounted crane, built in the late 1880s. In its early days it was used by Walter Sargent. Between the 1950s and 1990s it operated intermittently as a slipper factory. Now converted to apartments.

358 Former Walter Sargent shoe factory, Crabb St, Rushden

359 Former Wm Green shoe factory
SP 959663 ★ C

On High St South adjacent to Albion Place and opposite the junction with Wymington Rd, ¼ mile south of the town centre. This factory of three storeys plus basement was built in 1874 for William Green. The frontage is buff brick, the remainder red-brick. Distinctive stone motifs on the façade show shoes and shoe-making implements. Notable for the two-storey 'house' incorporated into the front of the building, sandwiched between the basement and top floor. Used by other shoe companies when Greens left for their present factory in Queen St in 1895 (Site 353), it is now all converted to apartments.

360 Former Wm Claridge shoe factory
SP 956665 ★

On the south-west side of Skinners Hill, immediately to the south of the parish church. Some parts of this large former shoe factory may originate from the 1860s. The three-storey frontage rebuilt in 1889 for Wm Claridge, is unusually of stone. It has two distinct parts, the right hand side has a shaped gable and the left is a mixture of ironstone and limestone.

361 Former Ritz cinema/theatre
SP 957667 ★ C

At the junction of College St and Alfred St in the town centre. The *Ritz* cinema, opened in 1936, was built to accommodate 1,200. It has a functional frontage of Bedfordshire red brick fairly typical of its time and it possessed the largest set of stage equipment in the county until the opening of Northampton's Derngate in 1983. It certainly had the largest stage - 71ft (23m) wide by 35ft (11m) deep. It is now used for bingo and films are occasionally shown in the unaltered circle.

362 Cast-iron milepost
SP 975638 ★

On the north-east side of the A6 Bedford Rd, just south of its junction

362 Cast-iron milepost, Bedford Rd, Rushden

with Avenue Rd. An 'L'-section cast-iron milepost set with its right angle facing the road and a triangular section filling the void on the top and set at approximately 45 degrees to the horizontal. Mileages shown are *Bedford 11, Rushden 2* and *London 62*. Thought to date from 1900-1910.

363 Ditchford river lock
SP 933682 ★

East of Ditchford Rd, which runs between the A45 and the B571 Wellingborough to Irthlingborough road. Ditchford Lock is on an artificial cut from the natural course of the River Nene. It has traditional beam gates at the upstream end but a steel curved gate at the downstream end, once typical of the locks on this stretch of the Nene.

RUSHTON   C3

364 Former Glendon & Rushton station
SP 844831 ★ LBII C

Adjacent to the bridge carrying the Midland Main Line over the road through Rushton village. The station, initially named *Rushton*, opened in 1857 on the Midland Railway's Leicester to Hitchin extension. The buildings

are of local limestone (c.f. former Desborough and Rothwell station - Site 102) with Norman-style decorated windows framed in polychrome brick. The gables have decorated bargeboards but the finials are missing. The name was changed to *Glendon & Rushton* in 1898. It closed to passengers in 1960 and has been deteriorating since then. A local group aims to purchase and convert it to a museum.

365 Glendon railway cutting
SP 854821 ★

Best viewed from the bridge carrying the minor road from the A6003 to Rothwell over the Midland Main Line, north-west of Kettering. A ¾ mile long cutting was dug for the construction of the Midland Railway in the mid-1850s. It exposed the iron ore strata, which led to extensive quarrying in this area over the next century. The Kettering to Manton line diverges from the mainline at this point, having been built in the 1870s. For over 100 years until resignalling led to rationalisation of the track, Glendon Junction formed the northern limit of the world's longest stretch of quadrupled track - the 75 miles from St Pancras.

366 Former houses for ironstone workers
SP 861836 ★

On the east side of the A6003 Kettering to Uppingham road, immediately to the north of the railway bridge at the junction with the Rushton to Geddington road. *Storefield Cottages* were built in the early 20thC by EP Davies for workers at its Storefield ironstone quarries. There are twelve brick cottages in two terraces of 6, and a pair of semi-detached foremen's cottages in adjacent Newton road.

SCALDWELL   B3

367 Remains of ironstone transfer point
SP 767723 ★

On the south side of the Scaldwell to Brixworth road, just outside Scaldwell opposite the entrance to Peters Lane. In what is now a builder's yard are the remains of two corrugated iron buildings used by the Staveley Coal

& Iron Co. from c1912 to 1962. The building with the curved roof to the left of the entrance was the workshop while the building to the right was the narrow gauge locoshed, though this has subsequently been rebuilt. Close-by were the facilities to transfer iron ore from the narrow gauge tramway which served quarries on the east side of the Scaldwell to Brixworth road, onto an aerial ropeway. The latter carried the iron ore down to sidings adjacent to the LNWR's Northampton to Market Harborough line just beyond Hanging Houghton, from just before WWI until 1954 (see also Site 218).

370 Remains of brick kiln, Spratton

SILVERSTONE B1
368 Former windmill
SP 674443 ★ LBII
Stands north of the road from Silverstone to Whittlebury. Built in the late 1820s, this red-brick, three-storey mill had a dome cap with fantail and carried four shuttered sails driving three pairs of stones for milling corn. The mill was complete when advertised for sale in 1897 but in 1904 the sails were removed to Wootton windmill. Standing as a shell for many years, the tower has now been converted to a dwelling.

SLAPTON B1
369 Former watermill
SP 644468 ★
On the River Tove, at the end of a track heading south-east from the Bradden road just west of its sharp turn at the east end of the village. The two-storey brick building with slate roof had a one-storey projection over the breast-shot water-wheel. Steam power was introduced in about 1880. Gristing continued until around 1950. The Midland Spice Company occupied the buildings in the 1960s but they are now a dwelling.

SPRATTON B3
370 Remains of brick kiln
SP 733707 ★
In a field adjacent to the north side of the Spratton to Brixworth road ¼ mile west of the Brampton Valley Way crossing, are the remains of an updraft kiln built between the wars. Only the bottom part remains with firing arches intact.

STANFORD-ON-AVON A3
371 Boundary markers & mileposts
SP 594779 ★ LBII
On the Stanford to Clay Coton road at the parish boundary, just north of where the road crosses over the A14. On each side of the road stand stone boundary markers. Of dressed stone, the square columns had ball finials although the one on the east post is now missing. The faces of each post have well-cut lettering giving distances, some to the half-mile, to nearby towns and villages.

372 Former Yelvertoft & Stanford Park station
SP 589784 ▢
¼ mile south of Stanford-on-Avon on the road to Clay Coton. The station, variously known as *Yelvertoft, Yelvertoft and Stanford Hall* (or *Park*) was on the LNWR's Rugby to Market Harborough line. Opened in 1870, it closed in 1966 and was converted to a dwelling. The wooden station buildings and

platforms remain but are difficult to see due to high hedges surrounding the property.

STANWICK — D3
373 Former railway bridge
SP 963712 ★
In Stanwick Lakes Country Park, ¼ mile west of the visitors' centre. This former railway bridge is on the trackbed of the former LNWR's Northampton to Peterborough line where it passed over a channel of the River Nene. It is constructed from cast-iron beams by the Brymbo Company.

STAVERTON — A2
374 Former toll-house
SP 553618 ★
Adjacent to the A425, ¾ mile north-east of Staverton village. Formerly on the Northampton to Warwick turnpike road, the former toll-house now suffers the indignity of life in a lay-by. It has a number of features which still readily identify its former role, principally the door diagonally across the angle formed by the 'L' of the original ground plan.

374 Former toll house, Staverton

STOKE BRUERNE — B1
375 Former Stoke Bruerne station
SP 736505 ★
On the west side of the Stoke Bruerne to Blisworth road, ¼ mile north of the junction with the Stoke to Shutlanger road. Stoke Bruerne station on the former Stratford and Midland Junction Railway opened in 1892 but closed to passenger traffic after only three months! The large station house remains as a dwelling.

376 Blisworth canal tunnel south entrance
SP 739503 ★ LBII
The south end of Blisworth tunnel on the Grand Union Canal (see Site 26) is reached by walking north along the tow-path from the village. On the east side of the entrance is an example of the large concrete ring segments used to line the middle third of the tunnel during its rebuilding in 1984. Also on the east side of the canal, behind the brick store sheds of 1908, is the incline of the track for taking the boat-horses over Blisworth Hill to pick up their boats at the other end of the tunnel.

377 Route of former tramroad
SP 738508 - 751488 ★
See also Site 27. From SP 738508 to 741501, the route of the southern part of the Blisworth Hill Railway was across fields to the east of the Blisworth road as it approached Stoke Bruerne. Boat-horses used the same route on part of the incline from the south entrance to the tunnel. The tramroad route diverged from the later boat-horse path about 50yds before it joined the tow-path, and can be identified by its level width for about 400yds on the gradual descent to near canal level. Between SP 744498 and 749492, the tramroad route is indicated by the very wide area, now occupied by a path, on the side opposite the tow-path. From SP 749492 to 751488, a track runs south from the A508, east of the canal crossing. After swinging towards the canal, the track joins the route of the tramroad which ends just south of the bottom lock (No.20). The wide area here was formerly the transshipment point between canal boats and the wagons running on the tramroad. The buildings alongside the bottom lock may have been associated with this wharf.

378 Canal museum
SP 743499 ○ LBII C
In the centre of Stoke Bruerne, on the east (tow-path) side of the canal, north of the road

bridge over the canal (Site 379). The Canal Museum, part of the Waterways Trust, occupies a former three-storey stone-built steam corn mill dating from soon after 1845. Displays cover construction, maintenance, operation and life on the canals, including clothes and traditional canal decorative painting. The shop has a comprehensive range of publications on canals and other inland waterways. Open Apr-Oct: daily; Nov-Mar: Wed-Sun. (www.stokebruernecanalmuseum.org.uk)

379 Double road bridge over canal
SP 744498 ★ LBII C
Carrying the road from the A508 through the village of Stoke Bruerne on two skewed brick arches, the west arch is the original bridge. The slightly larger east arch was added in 1835 when the locks were duplicated.

380 Top lock, Stoke Bruerne

380 Flight of canal locks
SP 743499 - 750489 ★ LBII C
Seven locks (Nos.14 to 20) change the level of the Grand Union Canal by 56ft (17m). The top lock is adjacent to the Canal Museum. To speed up traffic, in 1835 duplicate wide locks were provided on the east alongside each of the existing locks. In 1852 the original locks at the top and bottom of the flight were used to make side-ponds and the other five duplicate locks were filled in, although side-ponds were provided for the five original locks. These side-ponds went out of use during WW2 but still remain. Following the creation of the Canal Museum in 1963, the original top lock has been used to house a

boat-weighing machine, which had been used on the Glamorganshire Canal.

SULBY   B3
381 Canal reservoirs
SP 647809 ★ (car park)
The car park is located on the Welford to Naseby road, ¼ mile east of its junction with the A5199. Access to both dams is possible from the car park using the Jurassic Way. Sulby reservoir (the furthest from the car park at SP 652811) was built to feed the Leicester line of the Grand Union Canal and came into use on completion of the Welford canal arm c1814. Welford reservoir (SP 647809), immediately below Sulby reservoir, came into use in 1837.

SULGRAVE   A1
382 Former watermill
SP 556457 ★ LBII
The mill pond was fed from a spring and the tail-race and overflow became the head waters of the River Tove. The mill is just north-west of the village centre, east of the bridleway to Culworth, almost opposite the church. From the bridleway the mill appears to be only single-storey but its east side is three-storeys high at the north end where the internal 19ft (5.8m) diameter overshot waterwheel was situated. A Boulton & Watt beam engine was installed in 1788 (the first steam engine in the county) but was removed in the late 1790s. The large three-storey mill house, at right angles to the north end of the mill, carries datestones on the north and south sides. These refer to the birth and death of the person who left money to a previous owner of the mill and not to building dates!

383 Former windmill
SP 553459 ★
About ½ mile north-west of Sulgrave, close to the bridleway to Culworth. A three-storey stone-built tower mill with a very slight batter, its one pair of common and one pair of shuttered sails drove three pairs of stones for milling corn. Milling ceased c1885 and the mill became derelict until converted to be part of

384 Reservoir & former waterworks, Sywell

a dwelling in the early 1980s, with large extensions on two sides of the tower.

SYWELL   C2

384 Reservoir and former waterworks
SP 834650 ○
Now Sywell Country Park, the entrance to which is on the north-west side of the lane between the Earls Barton to Mears Ashby road and the Ecton to Sywell road. The reservoir and works were constructed by the Higham Ferrers & Rushden Water Board to supply those towns - about 10 miles distant. The works were completed in 1906. The nominal capacity of the reservoir was 236 million gallons and the water covers the site of Sywell watermill. The sand filters (now converted to gardens and a children's play area) were between the reservoir dam and the pump house. The latter is a brick building with restrained decoration and originally contained large gas engines driving the pumps. These were replaced by electrically driven centrifugal pumps. One of these, together with an elaborate water meter, was preserved in the pump house after the reservoir became a country park. A Heritage Trail explains the history and operation of the waterworks.

385 Sywell aerodrome and museum
SP 828678 ○
North-east of Sywell village, adjacent to the Sywell to Harrowden road. Sywell airfield came into being in 1928 as the base for the Northamptonshire Aero Club and saw service

as an RAF training airfield during WW2. Four different types of RAF hangar are represented and in use for various purposes: a blister hangar and examples of standard types B1, R1 and T2, although many have been re-clad, changing their wartime appearance. Sywell Aviation Museum with exhibits covering the history of aviation in Northamptonshire up to the end of WW2 is located in Nissen huts just inside the entrance.
(www.sywellaerodrome.co.uk/museum)

TANSOR   D4

386 Former windmill
TL 055910 ❑ LBII
Situated in the grounds of *Tansor Court*, about 150yds north-east of the church. A four-storey tower mill built of stone except near the top, which is of brick. It originally had an ogee cap. One pair of common and one pair of spring-shuttered sails provided power for two pairs of stones to mill corn. It seems to have been built c1830 and stopped work in the mid-1890s. After use as a water tower, the mill was gutted of all machinery in the 1950s and the cap replaced by a flat roof with a crenellated parapet. There is no public access but the top may be seen from the road to Fotheringhay.

TEETON   B3

387 Former watermill
SP 697696 ★
The mill stands on the west side of the road between Teeton and Holdenby and took water

from the Teeton Brook, a tributary of the Nene North Water. It is two storeys high, built of stone with the gable end facing the road, built of brick. The overshot water-wheel is still inside the mill; it is about 10ft (3m) in diameter and drove three pairs of stones until WW2. The mill is now called *Titon Milne*, the name given on a map of 1584 showing a mill at this site.

THORPE MALSOR   C3

388 Water trough
SP 835790 ★ C

On the east side of Church Walk close to its junction with The Square, stands an unusual stone water trough and well, said locally to be older than the Spanish Armada. It bears a strange inscription in Greek, calling on the passing traveller to offer a prayer on his way. A modern datestone bears the date 1589.

THRAPSTON   D3

389 Former corn exchange
SP 996787 ★ LBII C

On the north side of High St, between Chancery Lane and Oundle Rd. Originally the *George Hotel*, the Corn Exchange was established here in 1848, the hall being licensed to stage plays. In 1900 William Ebden Southam set up an auctioneer's business which operated from here for 100 years. The 2-storey, stone-fronted building has two classically inspired, but different doorways over one of which is a wooden horse-drawn plough and a carved limestone sheaf of corn.

390 Former Plaza cinema
SP 995786 ★

At the junction of Bridge St and Cosy Nook to the west of the town centre. The *Plaza Cinema* was built and opened in 1934. For a small (400 seat) cinema serving a small market town, its appearance, though plain, is not altogether displeasing. Although electricity was available in Thrapston by 1930, a Ruston Hornsby oil engine was installed at the cinema to meet its electrical needs. The *Plaza* closed as a place of entertainment in 1970 and is now a community facility.

391 Road bridge over River Nene
SP 991786 ★ LBII

At the western edge of the town, on the road to Islip, this nine-arched stone-built bridge, whilst dating from medieval times, has been much altered. Severe floods in 1795 swept away five arches and since then the structure has been widened using brick on its upstream side. The third and fourth arches from the Islip end retain pointed arches and mouldings however.

392 Name frieze from former ironworks
SP 994783 ★

In the north gable wall of 81 Midland Rd, at the junction with Foundry Walk. The original carved stone name frieze: *SMITH & GRACE SCREW BOSS PULLEY Co LIMITED* has been re-mounted in the end wall of one of the houses built on the site of the company's Neneside Ironworks which operated on this site from 1899 until 1995.

392 Name frieze from former ironworks, Midland Rd, Thrapston

393 Former railway viaduct
SP 994780 ★

Immediately north of the A14 road viaduct over the River Nene. It can be approached via a path or track from the old Kettering to Thrapston road in Islip. The nine-arch viaduct carried the Midland Railway's Kettering to Huntingdon line over the river until the 1960s. Built of blue brick and single track, it replaced the original structure in 1920.

TITCHMARSH   D3

394 Former watermill
TL 015809 ☐ LBII
On the River Nene and reached by a lane leading north-west from the A605, almost ½ mile north-east of the latter's junction with the road to Titchmarsh. A two-storey stone building with slate roof, the mill had six pairs of stones for milling corn. Some of these remain in-situ as does all of the unusual transmission arrangement including both great spur wheel and layshaft drives. The 13ft 6in (4.1m) diameter undershot water-wheel is in a dilapidated condition. The Middle Nene Cruising Club now occupies the mill which is on private property.

397 Telegraph/telephone cable junction marker, Watling St, Towcester

TOWCESTER   B1

395 Former Short Ashby motor car works
SP 691490 ★ C
Situated on the north-east side of Watling St at No.186, a little north of the police station on the opposite side of the road. Originally a Baptist chapel until bought by Victor Ashby for his pioneering Motor Works where he produced the Short Ashby motorcar. The baptistry providing for total immersion became the inspection pit. By the late 1920s, Victor Ashby

& Sons were electrical manufacturers. The premises are now occupied by MJ Gowling Ltd. dealing in carpets and flooring.

396 Former mint
SP 692487 ★ LBII C
On the south side of Park St, the 15thC *Old Mint House* is of two-storey rendered brick, slate roofed, with a huge chimney stack. Tradesmen's tokens were believed to have been minted here.

397 Telegraph/ telephone cable junction markers
SP 692488-693486 ★ C
Along the south-west side of Watling St are four cast-iron telegraph junction markers, similar to the one in Northampton (Site 255) but here the height varies slightly around 10in (25cm). On the boxes outside the *Saracen's Head*, 177 and 163 Watling St, the letters at the side of the crown are *V R,* whereas on the one outside No. 157 they are *G R.*

398 Former watermill
SP 694488 ★ LBII C
On a long leat from the River Tove, the mill complex is at the end of Chantry Lane, which leads north-east from the south (church) end of the Market Place. At the north-west end is the older three-storey mill, dated 1794, built of stone with a slate roof. During the early 1880s, roller mills were introduced and in 1895 an Armfield British Empire type water turbine was installed. The mill was completely gutted by a fire in 1911 and discoloured stone around some windows still provides evidence of this. The brick building with ironstone quoins alongside the tail-race is believed to have been built in the second decade of the 20thC whilst the even taller hexagonal brick building dates from 1937. Milling ceased after WW2. The buildings were subsequently occupied by a microelectronics firm and the turbine was restored to running order in 1997. The former mill house, across the yard from the mill, is early 19thC. Two-storeys high and 3 bays wide, it has 20thC extensions, including the porch which has a stone representation of a water-wheel above the doorway.

83

399 Wall-mounted cast-iron milepost
SP 694485 ★ C
On the south-west side of Watling St at No. 129 opposite The Lindens. A wall-mounted cast-iron plate, rectangular but with a curved top, with distances thus: *Stony Stratford 8 miles, Towcester 0 miles, London 59 miles*. This is a replacement plate, the original - removed during WW2 - is thought to have pre-dated the Holyhead Road style mileposts.

399 Cast-iron milepost, Watling St, Towcester

400 Former mineral water manufactory
SP 695484 ★ C
On the north-east side of Watling St at No. 36, a public house which used to be called *The Sun* but is now *The Monk and Tipster*. A two-storey building, of stone on the front to the road and on the north-west gable end, it has a wall crane to a first floor door in the gable. From this and extending along the Sun Yard is a two-storey brick extension of four bays. Francis Montgomery started manufacturing mineral water here c1877, using *The Watling Well* as a trade-mark embossed on the glass bottles. The business was taken over c1898 by Walker & Soames, brewers at Long Buckby. They built a warehouse and bottling area at No.95 across the street (next to the *Peacock Inn*) and the initials *W&S 1896* are visible on the wall of this building. They probably disposed of the business c1910 to CH Naylor

who continued to use *The Watling Well* trade-mark.

401 Towcester racecourse
SP 704477 ○
Adjacent to the A5, on the south-east edge of the town. The present course and its associated buildings were constructed in 1928 by the then Lord Hesketh. The Lodge Gates (LBII), one of the entrances to Easton Neston Park, are an outstandingly graceful example of early 18thC classical architecture and form an imposing approach to the racecourse. A somewhat surprising contrast is the 1997 grandstand designed by Francis Roberts of Lancaster. In 2005 the Empress Grandstand replaced the original 1928 wooden one.

402 Former cast-iron railway bridge
SP 685490 ★
On the trackbed of the former Stratford and Midland Junction Railway where it crosses the River Tove, north-west of the town. Can be accessed from the end of Belle Baulk, off Brackley Rd. A cast-iron rail bridge by Barwell of Northampton, originally constructed by the Northampton & Banbury Junction Railway. The bridge bears the date 1864 but the line was not opened until 1871. Although built to accommodate double track, the line was originally single as far as Greens Norton but in 1910 was doubled, carrying the lines for the Banbury and Stratford branches separately. Passenger services ceased by 1952 although freight traffic continued on the Stratford branch until 1964.

TWYWELL   C3
403 Former ironstone workings
SP 938772 ★
Part of Twywell Hills and Dales Country Park, accessed from the car park at the junction of the A510 and A14. Extensive remains of Islip Iron Co's Twywell Quarries stretch east from here towards Twywell village. Worked from c1900 to c1940, they have been largely left unrestored although some areas were planted with conifers. The final gullet and parallel waste tips have been cleared of trees and bushes and show the method of working.

403 Former ironstone workings, Twywell

UPTON B2

404 Water tower
SP 712611 ★ C
Situated south of Berrywood Rd, Duston in the parish of Upton, this tall water tower was built in 1876 in a vaguely Rhineland Romanesque style as part of the main block of Berrywood Asylum by Griffiths of Stafford. It subsequently became St. Crispin's Hospital which has now closed and the site is under redevelopment.

405 Former watermill
SP 721592 ★ LBII
Situated on the River Nene and reached via Upton Lane leading south from the new access road off the A45 Weedon Rd, ½ mile west of its junction with Upton Way. Can be seen from the bridleway which now circumvents the property. The stone three-storey building with a continuous slate roof was built in 1815. It housed the corn mill at the southwest end and the mill house at the other end. In 1841 Daniel Spokes was the miller, with his wife and 12 children. Little wonder that the Spokes family were associated with many of the mills in the county! The mill has been gutted of all machinery.

WADENHOE D3

406 Former watermill
TL 013834 ★ LBII C
On a long wide leat from the River Nene, this large two-storey stone-built mill with stone-slate roof is at the end of a lane leading south-east from the centre of the village. The building is distinguished by rows of cast-iron tie-plates (dated 1838) alongside the lintels of the upper storey windows on both up-stream and down-stream sides. A Gilkes Lunedale water turbine was installed in 1906. The building is now a private dwelling and, apart from the turbine and the sack hoist at the ceiling of one bedroom, is now devoid of any machinery.

WAKERLEY C4

407 Remains of calcine kilns and ironstone working
SP 947996 ★ LBII
Easily visible in a field between Wakerley and Barrowden (Rutland) are the remains of 4 calcining kilns built during WWI but never used. Cylindrical and about 33ft (10m) in diameter, the two completed ones are approximately 70ft (21m) high. The lower parts are of concrete, the upper parts of red

85

407 Remains of calcine kilns, Wakerley

brick, perforated by arches. Only the concrete bases of the other two were completed. Nearby are tramway embankments and the remains of a tipping dock adjacent to the former LNWR's Seaton to Wansford line. Bridge parapets are also visible on the Harringworth to Wakerley road, south of the kilns.

408 Former Wakerley & Barrowden station
SP 956997 ★

On the east side of the Wakerley to Barrowden road 200yds north of the village. Opened in 1879 on the LNWR's Seaton to Wansford line, the trackbed was on an embankment at this point. The station building was a wooden single-storey structure at rail level, built on an arched brick base. Since the station and line closed in 1966, the embankment at this point has been removed, leaving the station building stranded in mid-air. It is now converted to a dwelling although recent extensions somewhat lessen the impact.

409 Remains of limekilns
SP 960996 ☐

In dense undergrowth adjacent to the former trackbed of the LNWR's Seaton to Wansford line. Reached via a padlock-gated track off the Wakerley to Duddington road, ¼ mile east of Manor House Farm. The remains of three limekilns are visible, two set into the embankment, the third a free-standing brick-built kiln. At least nine kilns were in existence here by 1900, worked by Eldreds of Stamford.

WALGRAVE   C3

410 Former Walker shoe factory
SP 801722 ★

In Old Rd, Walgrave. The three-storey shoe factory was built for Stephen Walker c1900 (the adjacent house has a datestone: *SW – AD1899*). It was later used by George Webb as a shoe factory and then by the Regent Belt Co. Constructed of red brick, it has white brick banding and linings to the round-headed windows on the upper storey on both the west gable and south side. The north side has plainer red bricks and windows. The building is now converted to apartments.

WARMINGTON   D4

411 Former Eaglethorpe watermill
TL 074916 ★ LBII

This corn mill is on the southernmost of three loops of the River Nene and situated in the hamlet of Eaglethorpe, so is often called by that name. It is reached by a track running from the Warmington to Fotheringhay road just north of the A605 Warmington roundabout. A large, stone, three-storey, five-bay building, it has a lucam on the south gable end. The roof has been tiled, replacing the original slates. Built c1835 with four pairs of stones, eventually there were two, low, breast-shot water-wheels. The milling machinery and both water-wheels have been removed but the arches to the wheel-races are a distinctive feature of the upstream side of the mill. Now converted to a cooker showroom.

WATFORD   A3

412 'Pulpit' cast-iron railway bridge
SP 604699 ★

On the Jurassic Way footpath, ½ mile due north of Watford. This decorative cast-iron accommodation bridge carries the LNWR's Northampton to Rugby line and opened in 1881. At the 4 corners of the bridge are cast-iron refuges, which resemble church pulpits. It was ornate to compensate Lord Henley for the railway's intrusion.

413 Former goods shed
SP 597680 ★

On the south side of the B4036, about ¼ mile east of its junction with the A5, between the West Coast Main Line and the M1 motorway. The remains of the derelict brick-built goods shed are at the site of the former Welton

station on the London and Birmingham Railway opened in 1838. As late as 1900 the OS 25-inch map shows sidings which, via a wagon turntable, allowed transshipment between the railway and the adjacent Grand Union Canal.

414 Railway bridge over canal
SP 598679 ★

Taking the West Coast Main Line at an acute angle over the Grand Union Canal, 200yds south of the road bridge carrying the B5385 over the canal between Watford and the A5. Although the centre of this 200ft (60m) long bridge has been rebuilt with modern concrete beams, each end has 4 bays of shallow, brick barrel vaults supported by cast-iron beams. What appears to be the original 1838 London & Birmingham Railway façade also remains, with cast-iron beams in the Grecian Doric style ornamented with tryglyphs, supported on stone piers, with a cast-iron balustrade above.

415 Canal locks & side-ponds
SP 593686 - 593688 ★ LBII C

Reached along the tow-path, ½ mile north of the road bridge carrying the B5385 over the canal between Watford and the A5. The locks are on the Leicester line of the Grand Union Canal, from Norton Junction to Foxton, opened in 1814. Of the seven narrow locks (Nos.1 to 7) in the Watford flight, the four comprising the third to sixth form a staircase. The total rise is 52ft 6in (16m). The long side-ponds to the west are very extensive. Note also the cast-iron GJCCo. milepost (LBII) at the edge of the tow-path just below lock No. 2. From the top lock, with the M1 motorway behind and the sight of the canal, the A5 Watling Street and the West Coast Main Line in front, all within ¼ mile of each other, the influence of Watford Gap is apparent. North of the top lock the canal is level for a distance of 22 miles until the top of the Foxton flight in Leicestershire is reached.

414 Rail bridge over canal, Watford

WEEDON A2

416 Former toll house
SP 632598 ★

On the south-east corner of the A5/A45 road junction. The original two-storey building having the appearance of a toll-house, has been incorporated into the much larger and later building of the Crossroads Hotel. A diagonally placed door and Venetian window are clearly part of the toll-house but it is less certain if the bay window in the west elevation is part of the original design.

417 Main entrance to Weedon Depot

417 Remains of Royal Ordnance Depot
SP 629596 ❑ LBII*

Off Bridge St in Weedon Bec, accessed from the A5 Watling St. This spectacular site was laid out by the army from 1804 onwards when fear of a French invasion was strong. Weedon Depot was the first inland central store and distribution point for small arms, ordnance and other equipment. It had its own branch off the Grand Union Canal and later it had railway access from the London & Birmingham Railway. Specific areas are outlined below.

Ordnance canal basin (SP 631597 ★ C)
On the west side of the Grand Union Canal, a little north of where the canal is carried over the road from the A5 into Weedon Bec is the entrance basin for the ¾ mile long Ordnance Canal constructed in 1806. In 1838, the basin was reduced in size to allow the London & Birmingham Railway to cross. It is now used by a boat hire business.

Main entrance (SP 629596 ★)
The canal has been filled in between the basin and this point but is in water where it enters through an arch in the gatehouse built in 1812. Under the arch can be seen the original two-section wooden portcullis which could be used to close off this entrance. The gatehouse itself is a two-storey yellow brick building with a very shallow hipped slate roof, edged by a low parapet. It is surmounted by a wooden cupola presenting a clock face to the interior of the depot but louvred portholes to the public side.

Main compound (SP 629596-625596 ❑)
A 12ft (3.6m) high brick wall surrounds the site, with regularly placed stiffening pillars and bastions at each corner. The canal runs 440yds between 2 rows of four massive storehouses. The large turning basin in the centre is still there but the two original bridges linking north and south sides have been replaced. The eight 2-storey storehouses each measure 160ft x 35ft (48.8m x 10.7m). The first storeys are constructed of stone with brick above and hipped slate roofs. They were built before 1810 to store muskets brought in by canal from the small arms manufactories in Birmingham and are now used as private workshops and stores. At the far end of the main depot, a second gatehouse is in a dilapidated condition. Beyond this the canal was filled in c1920. There is no public access to the site but much can be seen by looking through the main entrance.

Magazine compound (SP 625596-621596 ❑)
The canal used to continue to the second compound which also has entrance arches protected by portcullises. This compound also built c1810, houses a series of substantial thick-walled, lightweight-roofed gunpowder magazines separated by earth-filled blast houses. These were built to store 10lb barrels of gunpowder. They are also in private use now. There is no public access to the magazine compound but it can be viewed from above, on the side road that leaves the A45 at the top of the hill out of Weedon on the way southwards (SP 625599).

418 Road/canal/railway in close proximity
SP 632598 - 631596 ★
Geographical constraints dictated the juxtaposition of road, rail and canal. They run parallel within a few hundred yards of each other at Weedon. Best seen by walking along Bridge St between the A5 (Watling St) and Weedon Bec. Watling St has been an important route through the county since Roman times and Weedon was a coaching stop in turnpike days. The 1796 Grand Junction Canal, is carried on a high embankment at this point across the Nene valley. The canal is level with the upper parts of Weedon church. Bridge St passes under the canal by means of a tunnel. The London and Birmingham Railway was the first public railway in the county and opened in 1838. Bridge St passes under it, barely 50yds past the canal. Weedon viaduct (LBII) 400yds further south-east at SP 633592, carries the line over Church St on five brick arches. All three routes continue in close proximity for several miles through the Watford Gap, with the addition of the M1.

WELDON   C4
419 Remains of stone quarrying
SP 925893 ★
On the west side of Kettering Rd just south of the triangular junction with Corby Rd and High St, *Haunt Hill House* (LBII C) is a fine example of a house constructed of Weldon stone. It was built in 1643 by master mason Humphrey Frisby and bears the Arms of a Mason's Company in the gable of the porch. Weldon stone was arguably the county's most important building stone from medieval times, used in a variety of buildings around the country (for example the fan vaulting in King's College, Cambridge). There is evidence of medieval quarrying in the vicinity of the village but the more extensive quarries and underground workings were largely obliterated by later ironstone quarrying and restoration.

420 Former brewery
SP 926895 ★ C
On the north side of High St approx.100yds west of its junction with Oundle Rd. A stone-built block, U-shaped in plan, with slate roof and hipped gables onto the street. At the base of the U is a three-storey brewhouse with pyramidal roof surmounted by a ventilator with a clock face to the front. Thought to date from the 18thC and probably the site of the Weldon Brewery operated by Thomas Wade in the early 19thC. Now in part commercial and part domestic use.

WELLINGBOROUGH   C2
The footwear trade began to expand in the early 19thC, evolving into the factory system some 50 years or so later. The LNWR's Northampton to Peterborough line came in 1845 but the arrival of the Midland Railway's Leicester to Hitchin extension in 1857 had a greater impact. Its earthworks revealed the extent of the ironstone deposits and the first blast furnaces on the Northamptonshire ironstone field were established in the town in 1853. The Midland Railway also constructed large locomotive sheds and marshalling yards here, being mid-way between London and Derby. A number of foundries were established, one producing motor engine blocks for Morris Motors and its successors until the 1980s. Two medium sized breweries came and went as did a large clothing manufacturer but significant remains of the gasworks are extant.

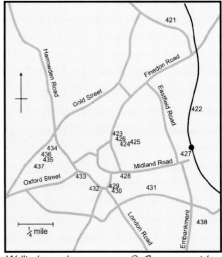

Wellingborough   *© Crown copyright*

421 Former blowing engine house for ironworks
SP 901695 ★
On the Finedon Rd Industrial Estate at the junction of Rixon Rd (A510) and Bevan Close. A large concrete building – originally painted blue but now re-clad in green and grey and named *The Powerhouse* – was the blowing engine house for Wellingborough (Rixons) Ironworks when the site was remodelled in 1934. Together with the brick retaining wall behind it, the structure is the only remaining evidence of the ironworks that closed in 1961, having operated on the site since 1885.

422 Former locomotive roundhouse
SP 904685 ☐
Off Mill Rd to the east of the Midland Main Line. The brick-built former locoshed, dates from 1872. It was one of a pair of round-house sheds used to house the mainly freight locomotives based at Wellingborough until the 1960s. It has been re-roofed and is used as a warehouse.

423 Cast-iron gateposts for former ironworks
SP 895683 ★
At the junction of Cannon St and Thomas St, north-east of the town centre, forming one of

423 Gateposts for former ironworks, Cannon St, Wellingborough

the entrances to the Waendel Sports Centre. Ornamental cast-iron gateposts mark the location of the entrance to Thomas Butlin & Co.'s East End Ironworks, which operated on the site between 1853 and 1876. It was the first blast furnace to be built in the Northamptonshire ironstone field.

424 Former Rudlens shoe factory
SP 896681 ★
At the junction of Mill Rd and Strode Rd is a 3-storey plus basement red-brick factory constructed in 1898 for Rudlens. The corner entrance has stone banding and a decorated gable above. There is an oriel window at first floor level. It was taken over by Sudborough & Wood in 1936 and was in use as a closing room as late as 1972.

425 Former Walker Bros. shoe factory
SP 896681 ★
At the junction of Mill Rd and Thomas St is the 9 bay, 3-storey factory constructed in 1890 for Walker Bros. It is of red brick except for the bay containing the loading doors which is of blue brick. In common with the adjacent Rudlens factory, it has an oriel window at first floor level. Now converted to apartments although the white plastic windows are not entirely sympathetic.

426 Former Watts & Co. leather factory
SP 896682 ★
In York Rd, a 3-storey plus basement factory constructed c1893 for Watts & Co., curriers and leather dressers. The window openings at ground floor level have segmental arches, those on the upper two floors are rectangular to take pivoting windows. Now converted to apartments but with disappointing white plastic windows.

427 Wellingborough station and former goods shed
SP 903681 ★ LBII
On the Midland Main Line from St Pancras to Sheffield, the station is reached from the town centre via Midland Rd. Opened in 1857 on the Midland Railway's Leicester to Hitchin extension, it was known as *Wellingborough*

(Midland Road) until the former LNWR's *London Road* station closed. The station buildings are of red brick with Norman style decorated windows lined in polychrome brick. Blind arches reflect the same design. The restored roof features decorated bargeboards and finials on the gable ends. The canopy to platform No.1 is supported by decorated cast-ironwork. The former goods shed adjacent to the station is of similar style and contains its hand cranes.

429 Wellingborough Museum, Castle Lane

428 Former Higgins stonemason's workshops
SP 896678 ★
In Midland Rd, 100yds west of its junction with Castle St. Impressive stone showroom/office with circular stone frontage and bay window and workshops to the rear was built for TH Higgins, stone-masons who were established on the site in 1866.

429 Wellingborough Museum
SP 895677 ○
In Castle Lane adjacent to the Castle Theatre to the south-east of the town centre. This rectangular red-brick building was constructed in 1892 as Dulleys swimming baths with the water heated by steam from the adjacent brewery (now demolished). The pool was filled in and it was converted to a two-storey shoe factory for Geo J Cox Ltd. during WWI under the name *Castle Works*. Cox's used it until 1995 and after being derelict for some time, it now accommodates Wellingborough Museum, with a section of the former swimming bath revealed, and exhibits covering the footwear and ironmaking industries. (www.wellingboroughmuseum.co.uk)

430 Former cattle market buildings
SP 896677 ★
Now incorporated into the Castle Theatre complex, immediately south-east of the town centre. The cattle market moved to this site in 1905 and the beautifully designed and well-built range of halls, rooms and superintend-

ent's house, remain virtually as constructed from the outside. It is of typical Edwardian red brick design, with stone string course and plenty of decorative features. The former main hall now forms the theatre's studio performance space.

431 Castle Fields bandstand
SP 899676 ★
Approached from Castle St, south-east of the town centre. Castle Fields bandstand constructed in 1913, whilst of typical 8-sided design, is of particular interest due to its classical style and the sophisticated use of a domed, reinforced concrete shell roof, designed by Richard Johnson, Clapham & Morris Ltd., reinforced concrete engineers. It has been subject to vandalism and is awaiting restoration.

432 Former Sharman shoe factory
SP 893677 ★
On the west side of Sheep St, just north of its junction with Doddington Rd. An early shoe factory or more probably warehouse c1850, of three storeys and 6 bays, built of stone for Nathanial Sharman. The owner's house is at the northern end of the range. The ground floor is now shops.

433 Entrance to former Silver Cinema
SP 891678 ★ C
On the west side of Silver St in the town centre. The *Silver Cinema* opened to film-goers in April 1920, seating almost 700. Local

436 Iron kerb, Buckwell End, Wellingborough

architects Talbot, Brown and Fisher provided an impressive red-brick frontage punctuated with stone string courses and cappings and dominated by a large semi-circular window in its upper portion, providing plenty of light to the café. Refurbished following a serious fire in 1951, the *Silver* closed 6 years later. Two shops occupy the Silver St frontage but the auditorium was demolished in 2005.

434 Former JC Coldicott leather factory
SP 887681 ★
On the north side of Rock St to the north of the town centre. The large 4-storey brick-built factory was constructed in 1907 for JC Coldicott, leather suppliers.

435 Stone sets in road surface
SP 887680 ★
In Short Lane, as Rock St turns into it. The original stone sets are still in place and entirely without top surfacing. A little further south, the north end of West Villa has a similar surface but with drainage channels.

436 Iron kerbs
SP 887680 ★
At the junction of Buckwell End and Short St, cast-iron kerbs are still in place at the edge of the footpaths. Some carry the words *William-son & Co Makers Wellingborough*. The firm's foundry was at the end of Midland Rd, near the entrance to the railway station forecourt and operated from 1865 until 1963.

437 Bassets Close bandstand
SP 886679 ★
Visible from within Bassets Close, approached from Westfield Rd or Barnabas St. This band-stand, like its near neighbour in Castle Fields

(Site 431), is chiefly of interest because of its roof. It is of an elaborate, timber-framed design and, whilst currently covered with asphalt sheeting, was originally clad with red clay tiles supplied by S&E Collier Ltd. of Reading. The uprights, balustrades and decking were all originally of timber construction but as a result of sustained vandalism have over the last 25-30 years been replaced with steel and concrete.

438 Former gas works
SP 904673 ★
At the end of Nene Court, on the east side of The Embankment, a short distance south of its junction with Irthlingborough Rd are buildings originally constructed for the Wellingborough Gas Light Co. Ltd. The company was founded in 1833 but the original works were not on this site. Construction of the *New Works* started in 1901 and came on stream in 1904. The buildings are of red brick, with slate roofs and round-headed cast-iron window frames. Behind is a tall round chimney of brick. Nearby, to the west is the former pump house, taller than the other buildings, with a hipped roof.

WEST HADDON · A3
439 Milestone
SP 631718 ★
On the south side of the A428, attached to an antique shop, opposite and slightly south of the *Pytchley Hotel*. This is a Northampton-shire sandstone milestone measuring approx. 3ft x 1ft 6in x 6in (1m x 0.5m x 15cm) in a semi-dressed state. A modern plaque fixed above it informs the reader that the wording: *Northampton 11 miles, London 77 miles,* was deliberately obliterated in WW2.

WHILTON   B2

440 Canal houses
SP 618643 ★ LBII C
On the east of the Grand Union Canal, just south of the bridge for the Whilton to Norton road, and alongside lock No.13. A row of two-storey brick-built houses with slate roofs. Between the two nearest the bridge, is an arch through which an inclined passageway runs, formerly to stables at the rear. A similar arch runs between the next two houses, the south-ernmost was once the *Spotted Cow* pub.

440 Canal houses, Whilton

441 Canal locks
SP 618643 - 616649 ★
Reached by the tow-path from the road between the A5 and the village of Whilton. These are the bottom four locks (Nos.10 to 13) of the Whilton and Long Buckby flight, built by the Grand Junction Canal Co. in 1796. The four have a total fall of 36ft (11m). All had single side-ponds built in 1805 to save water, some 60 years later converted to double side-ponds, in order to save more water. They went out of use in 1929, when steam traction engines were introduced for back-pumping water around each lock. Today, a single electric unit housed in a small building below Lock No.13 pumps water all the way from the bottom to the top of the flight. The side-ponds of this lock have been filled in but all the others are still in water and some remains

of paddle gear can be seen. Those at Lock No.12 have been cleaned out and it is possible to differentiate between the brickwork of the two construction periods. An interpretation board for the flight has been provided for visitors at Lock No.12, adjacent to the road. For the other locks in the flight see under Long Buckby and Norton.

WINWICK   A3

442 Former watermill
SP 628735 ★ LBII
On the Winwick Brook, a tributary of the River Avon, the corn mill is on the west of the lane between West Haddon and the village. The three-storey mill and adjoining mill house are of red brick with a slate roof. The overshot water-wheel was fed from a pond of about half an acre held by a dam on the west side of the mill. The three pairs of stones and much of the transmission machinery were retained when the mill was converted to a dwelling in 1990. However, the site has since been divided into three separate dwellings with a completely new access to the former mill house, cutting across the overflow channel from the mill pond.

WOLLASTON   C2

443 Museum
SP 908629 ○ C
In the former 1752 Congregational chapel in High St, behind the old Post Office. The displays include tools for crafts such as lace-making and footwear. (tel: 07804 241430)

444 R Griggs & Co. shoe factory
SP 907630 ★ C
On the south-west corner of the junction of High St with Cobbs Lane. A range of buildings, some dating from the mid-19thC, are the premises of R Griggs & Co. who have manuf-actured footwear on this site since the early 1900s. In 1959 they obtained an exclusive licence to manufacture Dr Martens boots. The site now serves as the headquarters of

Airwair International, the company set up by R Griggs to market the Dr Martens brand world-wide.

445 Former shoe outworkers' workshops
SP 905626 ❑ LBII
Behind 26-38 London Rd, a range of two-storey workshops, brick with slate roofs, originally used by shoe outworkers and dating from the late 19thC.

446 NPS shoe factory
SP 909628 ★
In South St at its junction with Holyoake Rd. A functional single-storey factory with northern rooflights dating from the early 20thC. There is a small concession to stone decoration around the office door and the gable above it. The Northamptonshire Productive Society formed in 1880, now known as NPS (Shoes) Ltd., still occupies the site.

WOODFORD   C3

447 Former Upper watermill
SP 973752 ★ LBII
Situated on the north-east side of the road between Great Addington and Ringstead is the survivor of two mills on the River Nene in Woodford parish. Its earlier names were

Willicoat, Willywater, and *Willy Wat* in 1844 when one water-wheel was driving three pairs of stones. By 1889 there were two, low, breast-shot wheels driving four pairs of stones and other machinery. It has been a corn mill, also a fulling mill, then a paper mill and later a bone mill. The two-storey mill is of banded Northampton sand ironstone and limestone. On the north-east side, at the end nearest to the river, weatherboarding instead of a stone wall indicates the drying area when paper was made here. There are remains of the two water-wheels, one inside at the north-west end and the other outside the south-east end, and some of the milling machinery remains.

448 Former water tower
SP 943760 ★
On the south-west side of the Cranford to Great Addington road, 600yds south-east of its junction with the A510. A stone built water tower approximately 15ft (4.5m) square and 15ft (4.5m) high with classical features, built to supply water to nearby Woodford House.

WOODFORD HALSE   A2

449 Former Farndon watermill
SP 533517 ★ LBII
On the River Cherwell on the north side of the road between West Farndon and Eydon. This two-storey stone mill, originally with red tile roof, had a Poncelet-type undershot wheel situated inside the west end of the building driving three pairs of stones. The mill cottage, also of stone, adjoined the east end of the mill. The water supply to the mill was reduced in 1899 when the Great Central Railway took water for its locomotives at Woodford Halse from the same brook upstream of the mill. Through an out-of-court settlement the GCR agreed to pay the mill owner £40 a year provided he continued to grind corn. The mill has now been converted to a dwelling and has been re-roofed in slate.

449 Former Farndon watermill, Woodford Halse

450 Former railway landscape
SP 540516 and others ★

The village of Woodford Halse was declining in the early 1890s when the Great Central Railway decided to make a junction with the Stratford and Midland Junction Railway here and to build a locoshed and freight yard. The population expanded from 500 to 2000, making it a railway town. However, all lines closed in 1966 and the tracks were lifted, leaving only the trackbed, triangular junctions, cuttings and bridges largely intact although they become more overgrown as time passes. They are best viewed from the over-bridges on the Woodford to Eydon road at SP 540516 (a pocket park covers part of the trackbed here) and at SP 541519. Part of a platform is visible above the road bridge at SP 540525. There is little visible sign from the Jurassic Way behind the industrial estate (SP 542532) of the site of the former locoshed and yards. The former Railwayman's Club, however, still exists at the junction of Hinton Rd and Station Rd (SP 537524).

452 Former blacksmith's forge, Yardley Hastings

YARDLEY GOBION   B1
451 Former canal wharf
SP 767453 ★

Located along a private track off the A508, opposite the turn for Yardley Gobion village but best viewed from the Grand Union Canal tow-path. Buildings survive within the walled area of the old wharf, including a two-storey stone warehouse of c1800 (LBII), with a slate roof and red brick inserts for the arches above windows and doorway. Now converted to a dwelling.

YARDLEY HASTINGS   C2
452 Former blacksmith's forge
SP 866568 ★ C

On the east side of High St just south of the junction with Little St is a single-storey stone building with a single window on to the road. This was formerly the forge and at its south end is a large arched opening into what used to be the shoeing shop. Past this, the drive goes into a yard on the north side of which is a range of dwellings and on the south a range of single-storey buildings associated with blacksmithing and wheelwrighting. The walls enclosing a narrow space at the end of this range provided an area for heating iron tyres to expand them to fit over wooden wagon wheels.

YARWELL   D4
453 Former watermill
TL 074973 ★ LBII

On a branch of the River Nene, the mill is at the end of a lane heading east from Mill Rd between Nassington and Yarwell. This lane is not a public right of way but the Nene Way footpath heading SSE from Yarwell crosses the river near the mill. A large three-storey stone mill, it was built in 1839 and worked until WW2 after which the machinery was removed and the building used for grain drying and storage.

YELVERTOFT   A3
454 Contour canal
SP 597731 - 622766 ★ C

From ½ mile north of the A428, east of Crick, to its crossing of the Yelvertoft to Elkington road, the Leicester line of the Grand Union Canal is a good example of the convoluted course of a canal which follows the contours to avoid expensive engineering. It crosses the Yelvertoft to West Haddon road three times in less than a mile and takes 5½ miles to travel the straight-line distance of 2¾ miles.

INDEX OF SITE NUMBERS

Aviation features   385

Canal features
Bridges/aqueducts   6, 36, 37, 74, 75, 78, 131, 228, 379
Buildings   39, 41, 42, 44, 45, 46, 226, 378, 440
Locks   47, 77, 227, 307, 314, 339, 380, 415, 441
Reservoirs   29, 43, 93, 94, 235, 381
Route features   6, 8, 23, 25, 35, 38, 40, 77, 313, 418, 454
Tramroads   27, 76, 377
Tunnels   26, 48, 87, 88, 95, 376
Wharves   7, 76, 86, 451

Distribution & retail of goods
Cattle market buildings   181, 299, 430
Market buildings/shops   250, 340, 389
Other   2, 245, 302, 417

Entertainment & leisure industries
Cinemas/theatres/galleries   177, 179, 183, 187, 241, 242, 252, 361, 390, 433
Parks   203, 207, 292, 431, 437
Sports   120, 164, 276, 401, 429

Extractive industries
Brickworks   60, 97, 141, 152, 330, 370
Iron furnaces   70, 71, 72, 114, 171, 219, 236, 421, 423
Ironstone quarries/mines   67, 83, 114, 118, 122, 132, 157, 170, 175, 218, 220, 229, 230, 231, 237,
308, 344, 366, 367, 403, 407
Limekilns   80, 330, 409,
Stone/gravel/slate   16, 20, 69, 139, 147, 419

Food & drink industries
Baking   115, 200, 290
Brewing & malting   73, 186, 210, 233, 234, 247, 248, 309, 315, 317, 318, 319, 320, 321,
420
Flour milling   3, 12, 13, 15, 18, 19, 21, 30, 31, 49, 52, 56, 58, 65, 68, 79, 89, 106, 107,
119, 121, 129, 135, 146, 151, 154, 155, 167, 172, 211, 215, 216, 224,
239, 325, 329, 368, 369, 382, 383, 386, 387, 394, 398, 405, 406, 411,
442, 447, 448, 453
Mineral water   400

Manufacturing industries
Boots & shoes   98, 99, 109, 110, 111, 123, 153, 158, 162, 188, 190, 191, 192, 193, 194,
195, 196, 198, 205, 206, 221, 222, 256, 257, 261, 262, 263, 266, 267,
268, 269, 271, 272, 274, 275, 277, 278, 279, 280, 281, 282, 283, 284,
285, 286, 287, 288, 289, 310, 336, 343, 345, 346, 347, 351, 353, 357,
358, 359, 360, 410, 424, 425, 429, 432, 444, 445, 446
Boot & shoe mercers   243, 332

FURTHER READING

GENERAL

Palmer, M & Neaverson P   *Industrial Landscapes of the East Midlands,* Phillimore 1992

Riden, P   *Catalogue of plans of proposed canals, roads, railways and other public works ...... in the Northamptonshire Record Office,* NRO 2000

Starmer, GH   *Industrial archaeology in Northamptonshire,* Northampton Museums & Art Gallery 1970

Various authors   *Victoria History of the Counties of England – Northamptonshire, Volume VI – Modern Industry,* Boydell & Brewer 2007

Various authors   *Northamptonshire Past & Present* contains many papers of IA relevance - see website or printed index, Northamptonshire Record Society 1948 to date

Wright, WB   *Seventy Five Years History,* Northampton Co-operative Society Ltd. 1945

EXTRACTIVE

Golby, F   *The Iron Ore Fields of Northampton from 1855 to 1921,* Author 2002

O'Rourke, R   *Some Northamptonshire Brickworks,* Bulletin of IA in CBA Group 9, No.13 July 1970

Sanders, J   *The story of Ironmaking In Northamptonshire 200BC - 1980AD,* Author 1994

Scopes, F   *Development of Corby Works, Stewarts & Lloyds Ltd. 1968*

Starmer, GH   *Northamptonshire Ironworks,* Bulletin of IA in CBA Group 9, No.11 Jan 1970

Sutherland, DS   *Northamptonshire Stone,* Dovecote Press 2003

Tonks, EH   *Ironstone Quarries Of The Midlands - History Operation & Railways, Parts I – VII,* Runpast Publishing Cheltenham 1988 onwards

MILLS AND MILLING

Stainwright, TL   *Windmills of Northamptonshire,* Wharton 1991

Starmer, G H   *A Checklist of Wind and Watermills in Northamptonshire,* Bulletin of I A in CBA Group 9 No.12 April 1970

TEXTILES

Bartlett, E   *Lace Villages – The Bobbin Lacemakers of Bucks, Beds & Northants,* Batsford 1991

Bates, D   *Cotton Spinning in Northamptonshire,* Northamptonshire Past & Present 1996/7 & 1998

Rowley, P   *Art, Trade, or Mystery – Lace Making in Northamptonshire,* The Lace Guild 2000

BOOT & SHOE

Cooke, J; Hilsden, K; et al   *The Northamptonshire Boot & Shoe industry,* English Heritage 2000

Eason, AE   *Saint Crispin's Men,* Park Lane Publishing 1994
Hatley, VA & Rajczonek, J   *Shoemakers in Northamptonshire 1762-1911 – a Statistical
                                   Survey* (Northampton Historical Series – 6), Authors 1971
Morrison, KA & Bond, A   *Built to Last – The Buildings of Northamptonshire's Boot and
                                   Shoe Industry,* English Heritage 2004
Mounfield, PR   Website with articles relating to the Northamptonshire leather
                                   and boot & shoe industries: www.mounfieldpublications.com

ENGINEERING
Bassett-Lowke, J   *Wenman Joseph Bassett Lowke,* Author 1999
Lee, M   *Henry Penn Bellfounder: from Peterborough to Pennsylvania,*
                                   Chapel House 1999
Middlemass, JL & Sawford, E   *William Allchin Ltd. Northampton* (British Traction Engine
                                   Builders No.1), Allan T Condie 1990
Starmer, GH   *A Checklist of Northamptonshire Foundries,* NIAG Newsletter
                                   No.4 Feb 1981 pp3-24
Watson, N   *Timsons – a Centenary History 1896,* Timsons Ltd. Kettering
                                   1996

FOOD & DRINK
Brown, M & Willmott, B   *Brewed in Northants: 2nd Edition,* Brewery History Society
                                   2010
Evans, J   *A Baker's Tale – The Story behind Oliver Adams Bakery,*
                                   Northampton Bakeries Ltd. 2000

DISTRIBUTION
King, J   *Weedon Royal Ordnance Depot Revisited,* Weedon History
                                   Society 1996

TRANSPORT
Blagrove, D   *The Railways of Northamptonshire,* Wharfside Publications 2006
Blagrove, D   *At the Heart of the Waterways – Canals in the Village of
                                   Braunston,* Buchebroc Press 2003
Blagrove, D   *Waterways of Northamptonshire,* Northamptonshire Libraries
                                   1990
Blagrove, D   *Two Centuries of Service – Canals at Stoke Bruerne and
                                   Blisworth,* Buchebroc Press 2005
Boyd-Hope, G; et al   *Railways and Rural Life - SWA Newton and the Great Central
                                   Rlwy,* English Heritage 2007
Child, JG   *British Bus Systems,* Northampton Transport Publishing
                                   Company n/d
Cossons, A   *The Turnpike Roads of Northamptonshire,* Northamptonshire
                                   Past & Present 1960
Faulkner, AJ   *The Grand Junction Canal,* WH Walker & Bros. 1993
Gibson, ML   *Aviation in Northamptonshire,* Northamptonshire Libraries
                                   1982
Hatley, VA   *Rails over Blisworth Hill 1800-1805* (Northampton Historical
                                   Series – 2), Author 1970

Irons, R & Jenkins, SC	*Woodford Halse – a Railway Community,* Oakwood Press 1999
Jordan, A	*The Stratford upon Avon and Midland Junction Railway,* Oxford Publishing Co. 1982
Mann, G	*Victorian Transport Schemes 1863-1900 – Trains Trams and Buses,* Author 1996
Phillips, D	*The River Nene from Source to Sea,* Past & Present Publishing 1997
Smith, G	*Northamptonshire Airfields in the Second World War,* Countryside Books 1998
Stevens, PA	*The Leicester Line,* David & Charles 1972
Various authors	*On The Move – A History of Road Transport in Northamptonshire, Vols 1,2 &3,* Rotary Club of Rushden Chichele, Thrapston and Raunds 1999/2001/2005
Warwick, R	*Illustrated History of United Counties Omnibus Co. Ltd., Parts 1-16,* Author 1997-2000
Waywell, R	*Industrial Locomotives of Buckinghamshire, Bedfordshire and Northamptonshire,* Industrial Railway Society 2001 (contains brief histories of many Northamptonshire firms)

SERVICES

| Richards, G | *Power in the Past* (Northampton Electric Light and Power Company), Electricity, May 1973 |
| Roberts, DE & Frisby, JH | *Northampton Gas Undertaking 1823-1949,* East Midlands Gas 1980 |

ACKNOWLEDGEMENTS

The Compilers wish to thank the following for their help in the preparation of this Guide: The Committee and Members of NIAG; Northamptonshire County Council Historic Environment Record, Northamptonshire Record Office, Northamptonshire Libraries; Northamptonshire Association for Local History; Brackley & District History Society, Daventry Local History Group, Finedon Local History Society, Flore Heritage Society, Long Buckby Local History Society, Roade Local History Society, Spratton Local History Society, Sulgrave Local History Society, Thrapston & District Historical Society, Weedon Bec History Society, Wollaston Heritage Society, Wolverton & District Archaeological & History Society, Eric Jenkins.

NORTHAMPTONSHIRE INDUSTRIAL ARCHAEOLOGY GROUP

NIAG is concerned with studying and promoting the county's industrial archaeology. It has been active for more than 40 years and has more than 100 members. NIAG aims to provide a forum for the exchange of information and views on industrial archaeology, to liaise with other bodies and to contribute to the management of industrial heritage in the county.

The Group has monthly indoor meetings, October to March, with speakers covering a wide range of topics and a programme of weekly outdoor meetings, May to August, visiting sites both inside and beyond the county boundary. A quarterly newsletter keeps members informed of activities and news.

For further information go to *www.northants-iag.org.uk* or contact NIAG Secretary: c/o Eastfields Farmhouse, Manor Rd, Rushton, Kettering, Northants, NN14 1RH